Classics

MILLWALL

FOOTBALL CLUB

Classics
MILLWALL
FOOTBALL CLUB

CHRIS BETHELL AND DAVE SULLIVAN

TEMPUS

First published 2002

Tempus Publishing Limited
The Mill, Brimscombe Port,
Stroud, Gloucestershire, GL5 2QG

British Library Cataloguing in Publication Data.
A catalogue record for this book is available from the British Library.

ISBN 0 7524 2705 9

Typesetting and origination by Tempus Publishing Limited
Printed in Great Britain by Midway Colour Print, Wiltshire

Contents

27 October 1990	Millwall 4 Sheffield Wednesday 2	Barclays League Division Two
26 January 1991	Millwall 4 Sheffield Wednesday 4	FA Cup fourth round
4 August 1993	Millwall 1 Sporting Clube de Portugal 2	The Opening of the Stadium
18 January 1995	Arsenal 0 Millwall 2	FA Cup third round replay
16 March 1999	Millwall 1 Walsall 1	Auto Windscreens Shield Southern Area Final Second Leg
7 April 2001	Millwall 4 Rotherham United 0	Football League Nationwide Division Two
6 May 2001	Millwall 5 Oldham Athletic 0	Nationwide League Division Two
1 January 2002	Watford 1 Millwall 4	Nationwide League Division One

Introduction

This joint effort in selecting fifty *Classic* matches has been an enjoyable exercise. Many Millwall supporters may feel that other games maybe worthy of inclusion have been overlooked, but we have attempted to cover most of the eras that the club has performed in.

So how do we define a classic match – exciting, memorable, or even unbelievable? We think we have covered most descriptions there are, and we hope that you will agree with us on the variety of matches chosen.

Attempts to locate details that we could relate on the early days of Millwall Rovers have been frustrated by the lack of coverage of the club, who on their foundation were no more than a parks side.

The majority of these games may show Millwall victorious, but this action is not meant to demean defeats as they too can be glorious – what fan doesn't remember the two fairly recent defeats at Wigan (both by 1-0), in which the Lions dominated the games only to leave with nothing.

Some of the encounters contained in the book are personal recollections, and others are from what has been gleaned by research, but whatever the game, the hope is that the Millwall supporter no matter how old can relive those games they have witnessed.

If you enjoy reading *Millwall Classics* as much as we have enjoyed writing and researching it, then the endeavour will have been worthwhile.

David Sullivan
October 2002

Acknowledgements

On behalf of Millwall FC Museum, the authors would like to thank the following individuals who have all been of great assistance in the compilation of this book: Brian Tonks, Graham Tonks and Dave Webster, the Millwall photographers over the past three decades, whose expertise in photography brings to life the history of Millwall in books. Richard Lindsay for his dedication in research into the history of Millwall and passing on the knowledge for publication. Richard Smart and John Davies for copying from their collections to enhance details on the matches. Billy Neil for his quotes. Also Eileen, Stacie and Sasha Bethell for all the typing and correcting I needed. Special thanks goes to all the supporters who have sent us photos and cuttings, thus supplementing the archives for this book, and the Millwall FC Museum. And to all at Tempus Publishing for their help in producing the three books.

OFFICIAL PROGRAMME
CHELSEA FOOTBALL & ATHLETIC CO., LTD.

Directors :

Lieut. J. H. MEARS, R.M. (Chairman)
J. E. C. BUDD (Vice - Chairman)
C. J. PRATT
H. J. M. BOYER
L. J. MEARS

Manager-Secy.—Wm. BIRRELL

17th MARCH, 1945. Price : ONE PENNY

FOOTBALL LEAGUE (SOUTH)
CUP COMPETITION SEMI-FINAL TIE

ARSENAL
(RED)

Kick-Off 3 p.m.

1
Sgt. MARKS, G.

2
MOODY, K.
(Grimsby)

3
Sgt. SCOTT, L.

4
BASTIN, C. S.

5
Cpl. HALL, F.
(Blackburn Rovers)

6
Sgt. HAMILTON, W.
(St. Bernard's)

7
Cpl. FARQUHAR, D.

8
A. N. OTHER

9
F/Lt. DRAKE, E. J.

10
L.A.C. MORTENSEN, S.
(Blackpool)

11
Cpl. WRIGGLESWORTH, W.
(Manchester Un.)

Referee—Lt.-Com. G. CLARK (London)

Linesmen

Mr. A. BOND
Blue and White Flag
Mr. W. CASLING
Red and White Flag

11
Cpl. MEDLEY, L. D.
(Tottenham H.)

10
L.A.C. BROWN, T.

9
Sgt. JINKS, J.

8
Sgt. BROWN, A. R.
(Charlton Athletic)

7
RAWLINGS, S.

6
TYLER, L.

5
SMITH, E.

4
LUDFORD, G.
(Tottenham H.)

3
Sgt. FISHER, G.

2
L/S DUDLEY, R.

1
Gnr. GREGORY, E.
(West Ham)

MILLWALL
(ROYAL BLUE)

MILLWALL ATHLETIC v. CHESHAM

9 September 1893
Athletic Ground, East Ferry Road

Friendly
Attendance: 1,500

This totally one-sided affair still constitutes Millwall's biggest ever victory in any shape or form, and might never have occurred if their original opponents had not cried off. Millwall had arranged a match against a unit of the Sherwood Foresters, but as they were required for military manoeuvres, it was poor old Chesham who filled in at the last minute.

Unfortunately, information on who the other goalscorers were has proved elusive so far, and the fellow charged with the task of reporting the game must have been bored by the time the interval was reached, and probably retired to the nearest public house. What is known is that it was nearly four o'clock when Spratley, the visiting centre forward, got the game underway. As events turned out, one would deem it necessary to ask if this was the only kick he had during the whole of the game? Parity disappeared after ten minutes when Arthur Wilson opened the floodgates with a nice shot, and from then until half-time Chesham were chasing shadows.

Freddie Hollands had an effort disallowed, but shortly afterwards Jimmy Lindsay opened his account to be followed in quick succession with efforts from Eddie Jones, Hollands, Wilson again before Peter Cunningham got in on the act; Jones and then Lindsay added to the tally, as the game was turning into a rout long before the interval.

Some contemporary reports of the game differ over the half-time score, the *East London Advertiser* states it was 10-0, and a Chesham paper gives it as 9-0 – whatever the true state of affairs, poor Chesham could hardly be blamed for thinking they might have been better off on manoeuvres with the Foresters; the bombardment could not have been any worse than they were taking on the Isle of Dogs.

If anything positive came out of this game, it was the marking of Millwall Athletic's progress as a club and the need to meet stronger opposition on a regular basis. Subsequently, Millwall took a prominent lead in resurrecting the idea of the Southern League, which had been shelved at the beginning of the 1890s, but was given a more favourable response this time around. After the formalities had been ratified, it led the club down the road to professionalism three months later, and full-time football in 1894.

Millwall Athletic, 1893/94. From left to right, back row: W. Lindsay, J. Graham, W. Davis, G. Aitken, J. Duke, J. Robertson, O. Caygill (captain), A. Roston Burk (referee). Front row: A. Wilson, E. Jones, J. Lindsay, W. Cunningham, F. Hollands.

Millwall Athletic 17
Wilson (3), Lindsay (4)
Cunningham (2), Jones
Hollands, A.N. Other (6)

Chesham 0

Referee: Mr S.R. Carr (Hotspur)

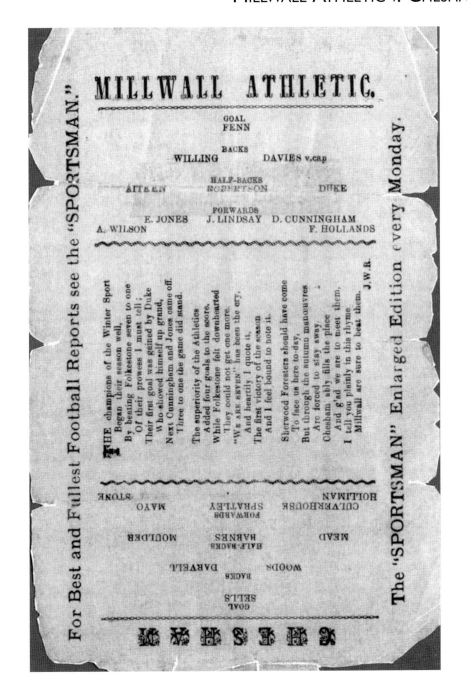

Millwall Athletic: O. Caygill, W. Davis, T. Willing, D. Aitken, T. Robertson, J. Duke, A. Wilson, E. Jones, J. Lindsay, W. Cunningham, F. Hollands.
Chesham: F. Sells, W. Woods, G. Darvell, A. Mead, H. Barnes, E. Moulder, W. Holliman, J. Culverhouse, F. Spratley, W. Mayo, H. Stone.

MILLWALL ATHLETIC v. TOTTENHAM HOTSPUR

19 September 1896
Athletic Ground, East Ferry Road

United League
Attendance: 6,000

This was the inaugural season of the United League, which came into being to supplement the Southern League and brought new opponents to East Ferry Road, with the likes of Loughborough, Wellingborough, Rushden, and (to renew acquaintances) Woolwich Arsenal. This particular meeting between another team of old London rivals was noted not just for the eleven goals that were scored, but also for the introduction of a substitute in a *bona fide* fixture, the best part of seventy years before the rule was introduced.

When Millwall skipper George King won the toss, little did he realise that a little piece of history was in the making, and when Spurs striker Billy Newbigging scored with a firm shot, and then with a lovely header, both within a minute of each other, the notion would have been the last thing on King's mind. Millwall then found themselves down to ten men when their Welsh international Joe Davies was injured in a tackle from Stan Briggs, who had played few times for Millwall in their amateur days. After Joe's departure, Briggs sportingly suggested that Archie McKenzie be allowed to replace Davies, which brought spontaneous cheering from the crowd.

With both teams now back at full strength, Millwall could concentrate on how to get back into the match. As they settled down Jack Calvey hit a shot on the run which flew narrowly wide, and he followed that moments later by another attempt when he fastened on to a loose ball, only for the referee to pull the game back for a Millwall free kick. If the Dockers fans felt hard done by with the decision, all was forgotten as Joe Gettins lashed home an unstoppable shot to reduce the arrears. Soon afterwards, Calvey thought he had equalised when he forced the ball into the Tottenham net but his effort was disallowed, and a free kick was awarded.

Spurs' riposte to this let off was to swarm around the Millwall goal in an attempt to lengthen their advantage before the interval. During this spell of pressure, Dave Robson effected a timely clearance to save the home side, and then Briggs hit a shot that went just over. The half was brought to an end when Newbigging clattered into Millwall 'keeper Tommy Moore.

Millwall's intentions at the start of the second half were quite clear, as Aitken, and then Whelan, tested Ambler in the Spurs goal. Ambler stayed amidst the action by charged Alf Geddes, which left the Millwall winger severely winded. It was left to Mickey Whelan to square the match at 2-2 when he drove home the resulting free kick.

The contest was already coming to the boil as Gettins really raised the temperature when he hedged Millwall in front for the first time, his hard shot along the ground beating Ambler to nestle nicely in the back of the net. Following this, Aitken's effort was blocked by John Montgomery to stop Spurs falling further behind, as Millwall began to grow in confidence.

Although Millwall were now dictating play, they allowed Tottenham to pull level through Harry Crump, much to the disgust of the home support. Undaunted, Millwall ripped into the attack, with Ambler having his work cut out to stem the tide of attacking play. Despite their dominance, it was Spurs who nearly scored in a breakaway move, only for King to save his side in the nick of time.

Millwall Athletic 6
J.H. Gettins (3),
Whelan, Calvey
Aitken

Tottenham Hotspur 5
Newbigging (2),
Crump, Clements,
Payne

Referee: Mr E.G. McDonald

Encouraged by this, Tottenham carried the play to the Dockers, and Moore had to be alert to a McElhaney drive, but with Whelan and Geddes foraging down the flanks Millwall began to enjoy their best spell of the game. It was a Geddes run down the left that engineered Millwall's next goal, when Calvey firmly headed home number four from his centre.

George Aitken had seemingly put Spurs to the sword when Ambler, who had denied him earlier with a splendid save, was beaten with a similar shot to register Millwall's fifth. However, Spurs' desire not to be outdone brought them back into contention when Greenwich-born Bob Clements scored the game's ninth goal with a well-placed shot.

When Ernie Payne grabbed Spurs' fifth goal with a really soft effort that barely crossed the line, most fans would have settled for a hard-earned draw, but directly from the kick-off Joe Gettins completed a well-earned hat-trick. Still the excitement wasn't over as both goals came under threat, with Graham and Briggs making fine interceptions for their respective teams. One final fling from Millwall just before the end came when Gettins broke away to send in a cross, which Whelan converted, only to see the flag had been raised for offside.

Millwall went on to win the United League, and so held the unique distinction of winning championships in this competition and the inaugural Southern League.

1896/97 (United League only)

P	W	D	L	F	A	PTS
14	11	1	2	43	22	23

Champions
Manager: Fred Kidd
Top Goalscorer: John Calvey (12)

Archie McKenzie was a Scottish inside-forward who came on as a substitute when Joe Davies was injured during the United League match against Spurs. This line drawing is a reproduction taken from a scrapbook from around the period.

Millwall Athletic: Moore, Graham, Robson, King, Aitken, H. Matthew, Whelan, Calvey, J.H. Gettins, Davies (McKenzie), Geddes.
Tottenham Hotspur: Ambler, Montgomery, Burrows, Devlin, Briggs, Crump, McElhaney, Milliken, Newbigging, Clements, Payne.

MILLWALL ATHLETIC v. WOOLWICH ARSENAL

16 January 1897
Athletic Ground, East Ferry Road

FA Cup fifth qualifying round
Attendance: 20,000

The prize awaiting the winners of this qualifying tie was a place in the first round proper, and Millwall entered the arena in a sombre mood due to the recent death of their trainer Bill Lindsay. As a mark of respect they wore black armbands on their changed strip of white shirts.

The Arsenal, after recently changing their name from Royal to Woolwich, drew a record attendance at the Athletic Ground, and an added incentive to the home team was the fact that their visitors were now established members of the Football League.

The game had been built up by the press in the days leading up to the encounter. As Arsenal got the match underway, those who had found room to report it, would not in their wildest dreams expect to see Millwall completely dominate the opening half the way they did. It was Archie McKenzie who opened the scoring after 23 minutes – which generated such a roar from the Millwall support that it seemed to embarrass poor Archie. But if that goal was good, what was to follow was even better, when Mickey Whelan's cross found fellow winger Alf Geddes, who slotted home number two on 35 minutes.

Millwall were now full of confidence and Arsenal had hardly any time to mount an assault on the home side's goal; it came as no surprise when Geddes added a third after 40 minutes following a splendid run. If Lions thought this strike would bury the Gunners, they were soon brought back down to earth when in the last three minutes of the half the Football League side reduced the arrears, not once but twice as Boyle, and O'Brien scored in quick succession.

The second half was a more even affair, with both Millwall and the Reds striving to obtain the advantage. It seemed that one goal from either side would settle the outcome one way or the other, with Athletic looking for the clincher, and Arsenal the equaliser. As it turned out it was Millwall's famous amateur J.H. ('Joe') Gettins who sealed the win for the home team, when he lost his marker to create himself some space and put away a superb shot that gave Leather no chance to stop Millwall's fourth. The Lions were in the next round.

This was an excellent team performance by Millwall, in which two individuals excelled, namely Gettins and his fellow forward Jack Calvey – who not only contributed up front but found time to drop back into midfield when deemed necessary. This result was a most satisfactory way to honour the memory of Millwall's late trainer.

Millwall Athletic 4	Woolwich Arsenal 2	Referee: Captain Simpson
McKenzie,	*Boyle,*	
Geddes (2)	*O'Brien*	
J.H. Gettins		

Millwall Athletic v. Woolwich Arsenal

Above: The Millwall team of 1896/97. From left to right, back row: J. Davies, G. Aitken, F. Thorne (director). Middle row: A.T. Millar, T. Moore, P. Robertson, A. McKenzie, H. Matthews, M. Whelan, J. Carter, A. Geddes, W. Lindsay (trainer). Front row: J. Graham, D. Robson, G. King, J. Calvey, J.H. Gettins.

Right: Alf Geddes, Millwall stalwart of the 1890s, who scored two in the game against Arsenal.

Season 1896/97

P	W	D	L	F	A	PTS
20	13	5	2	31	15	31

Southern League First Division
Second place
Manager: Fred Kidd
Top Goalscorer: John Calvey (17)
Average Attendance: 3,350

Millwall Athletic: Carter, Graham, Robson, King, Robertson, Matthew, Whelan, Calvey, J.H. Gettins, McKenzie, Geddes.
Woolwich Arsenal: Leather, Shrewsbury, Sinclair, Crawford, Boyle, Davis, Brock, Haywood, Meade, O'Brien, Russell.

MILLWALL ATHLETIC v. ASTON VILLA

5 March 1900
Elm Park, Reading

FA Cup second round (second replay)
Attendance: 20,000

This game that took place in the Royal County of Berkshire was to become a momentous occasion in the history of Millwall Football Club: not only would they progress to their first ever FA Cup semi-final, but in doing so they knocked out the current Football League champions at the third attempt.

Aston Villa were the first to show with an attack down the right flank that petered out. However, it was Millwall who settled down in a manner much more to their liking (calming the nerves of their many fans in the crowd who had taken full advantage of the cheap rail excursion to Reading). Millwall's forward line caught the eye in the opening stages, particularly the pace, power, and cleverness that Willie Dryburgh exuded when forcing George to concede a corner. Villa proceeded to twice come on strong down the left through Templeton, before the ball was again in the Villa area, where Spencer had to be at his best to stop Gettins and Banks in successive attacks. Then George had to react to Brearley's snapshot.

The exchanges were now favouring Millwall, whose pace was a constant threat to their more illustrious opponents on a perfect playing pitch. Despite this superiority, Walter Cox, the Millwall 'keeper, was forced to contribute to the Millwall cause by running out and clearing a through ball from Devey, before dealing with a dangerous effort from Templeton.

After 15 minutes of play, the Lions took the lead they deserved through a perfectly-flighted corner, from which Hugh Goldie's header set up Bertie Banks to finish off with a cracking drive that gave the goalkeeper no chance. Further forays into the Villa half were dealt with by the resolute Spencer, who foiled both Banks and Gettins, before the inevitable happened, a second goal for Millwall. This blow came within five minutes of the first, and it was Joe Gettins (who was given time off from his job as a Reading schoolmaster to play in the game) who did the damage with a run that easily tricked Evans, the Villa full-back, before crashing his shot past the astonished George.

Millwall were now buoyant, although Villa's reply was instant as they attempted to step up the pace of the game. The Midlands side were unfortunate when Templeton met Charlie Athersmith's centre on the full, with his drive cannoning off a post before being cleared. It was then Athersmith again who put the Millwall defence under more pressure with another tantalising cross, which Cox dealt with admirably.

Although Villa were coming back into the game, it was Millwall who looked the more likely to score again as the League Champions appeared to lack any killer instinct. However, as the interval approached, a mêlée in front of the Millwall goal caused some panic.

The break seemed to rejuvenate the Villa, who from the start of the second half did most of the attacking with Templeton being their most enterprising forward. It was their shooting that was letting them down, with Athersmith again failing in front of goal. The Lions, after being pulled up twice for offside, responded in kind, and when Gettins and Dryburgh combined in a forceful attack, Evans was forced to concede a corner.

Millwall Athletic 2
Banks
J.H. Gettins

Aston Villa 1
Johnson

Referee: J. Lewis (Blackburn)

J.H. Gettins, scorer of the second goal against Aston Villa in the 1900 FA Cup second round tie.

Millwall Athletic: Cox, Burgess, Allan, Smith, Goldie, Millar, Dryburgh, Brearley, J.H.Gettins, Banks, Nicol.
Aston Villa: George, Spencer, Evans, Bowman, Wilkes, Noon, Athersmith, Davey, Garraty, Johnson, Templeton.

MILLWALL ATHLETIC v. ASTON VILLA

Action from the game: Millwall defend a Villa corner.

George was brought into action on a couple occasions to clear his lines, but as Millwall started to tire the Villa were able to take some of the advantage. Whereas in the earlier phases of the encounter the laurels were awarded to the Dockers' attack, it was now the turn of Millwall defence to show their mettle, with the backs (Charlie Burgess in particular) coming into their own.

With less than ten minutes remaining, Aston Villa scored a consolation goal. Johnson received the ball after a previous attack had drawn the Dockers' defence out of position, setting himself up with an open goal that he gleefully took. The excitement was running high as Villa poured forward in search of an equaliser. Gettins was now a passenger on the wing, and only a fine interception by Dave Smith stopped Garraty from levelling the tie.

Still Millwall were not finished though, as the plucky Gettins managed to create a chance for Dave Nicol – who might have done better with it – but the in end it didn't matter as the referee blew his whistle for full time. Millwall would play Southampton in the semi-final, making this the first time two clubs from the Southern League had met at this stage of the competition.

1899/1900:

P	W	D	L	F	A	PTS
28	12	3	13	36	44	27

Southern League First Division
Seventh Place
Manager: Fred Kidd
Top Goalscorer: Herbert Banks (11)
Average Attendance: 6,821

ASTON VILLA, —V— MILLWALL.
LAST SATURDAY.

DRYBURGH MAKES SOME GOOD CENTRES.

RESULT.
ASTON VILLA 1.
MILLWALL 1.

WHELDON'S HEAD GETS THE ONLY GOAL FOR THE "VILLANS".

WELL PLAYED "DOCKERS"!!

GETTINS PUTS IN SOME TELLING WORK.

Millwall Athletic v. Southampton

24 March 1900
Crystal Palace, London

FA Cup semi-final
Attendance: 34,760

This match underlined the advance the professional game had made in the South, with these two clubs (both of which had been founded in 1885 and were founder members of the Southern League) competing in the penultimate stage of the FA Cup. For Millwall Athletic Football Club and its followers, this would be the greatest day in their short history.

On a perfect playing surface, it was the Saints who got the game underway, skipper Dave Smith having won the toss and electing to kick with the wind. Having gained possession, Millwall began to press through Gettins and Dryburgh, the attack being cleared at the expense of a throw on the Millwall left. This enabled the youthful Millar to create an opening with some splendid play, only for Dryburgh to commit a foul; from the resultant free-kick Milward, the Southampton outside left, took up the running before a fine interception by Smith snuffed out the danger to the Millwall goal.

The response from the Dockers was a swift move into the Saints' half by Banks and Brearley, which was halted when the latter was fouled; the free kick, taken by Charlie Burgess, came to nothing as play began to even out, and it was Milward who became a threat once more as he led the Saints attack. Cox in the Millwall goal was forced to concede a corner, which was cleared. This was followed by a move down the left wing by Banks, whose fine cross was dealt with by Robinson, before Millwall regained possession. When Dryburgh fouled yet again a melee took place, in which Burgess had an effort blocked before Smith's shot flew over the bar.

Alf Milward was Southampton's main hope of achieving something, and he set up Wood, whose long range shot was held comfortably by Cox. The game became something of a midfield tussle for the next few minutes, before Millwall broke with a move that involved Banks, Nicol, and Brearley. This was only stopped when Nicol appeared to foul, but the referee waved away any claims for a free-kick.

Despite this setback, Millwall won a corner, which caused panic in the Saints defence, but again they cleared the danger, before some excellent play by Millar sent Dryburgh away. His telling cross caused Robinson some concern before he cleared. Southampton then pressed the Dockers. Wally Cox twice averted danger, including another long-range strike from Wood, and Turner looked like scoring against the run of play until an Eddie Allan tackle saved the day. Millwall's response was a ground shot from Brearley that Robinson saved as Millwall tried to make the most of their superior possession.

Millwall did manage to get the ball into the net, but Allan's effort was ruled out, and then Banks had the opportunity to raise the spirits of the Millwall supporters with two attempts just before the interval. First, he made Robinson bring off a tremendous save from under the crossbar, and then after some lovely approach work by Dryburgh and Gettins, he skied the ball over the bar when well placed.

After the break, the Saints had the wind in their favour, but it was Millwall who showed the initiative when Gettins was fouled by Chadwick. However, the free kick came to nothing as Southampton powered forward for an attack in which Farrell was injured. After play resumed, the Saints looked a better proposition. Turner's fine cross was met by Chadwick, who seemed certain to score only for Burgess to pop up from nowhere to clear his lines.

Millwall 0   Southampton 0   **Referee:** A. Kingscott (Derby)

Clever Southampton forwards

Millwall's Burgess indulges in some mighty overhead kicks

Pretty head flay by Allan

Cox fisting out

A collision of heads 'Ouch'

Gettins gone away

Referee Kingscott besieged

Cartoon of the FA Cup semi-final at Crystal Palace, Saturday 24 March 1900, Millwall against Southampton.

Play was continually stopped, either for fouls or injuries, and fluent football was at a premium. When it did get going though, it was end-to-end, albeit without any actual scoring. Robinson was the busier 'keeper, although his opposite number, Cox, nearly gave away a goal when he completely missed the ball, but Yates put his shot over the bar when in front of an open goal.

Millwall's Hugh Goldie accidentally kicked Woods in the back, with many of the Saints fans urging Mr Kingscott to send him off. Then it was the turn of Banks to receive a nasty blow to the head, which required him to leave the field. Southampton utilised the extra man and attacked with a lot more vigour, with only Millar's intervention preventing Turner from giving them the lead. Sixty seconds later, Burgess repeated the feat, clearing a shot destined for the net. With Banks now back in the fold, Millwall attacked through him and Nicol, before Burgess again had to nip a Saints move in the bud as they attempted to counter through Farrell, Wood, and Yates.

As the game was nearing its conclusion, Cox denied Southampton a chance at the expense of a corner, but despite the injuries received by players on both sides, play was fairly bright as both teams vied for that illusive opening goal. It nearly came when Gettins tested Robinson with a fine shot. Southampton then forced three successive corners, before Allan became the latest casualty when he received a kick while clearing the ball.

Just before the final whistle, a last throw of the dice by the Saints in an attempt to reach the final was denied by the resolute Athletic defence, in which full-back Charlie Burgess was a colossus. As the referee brought the proceedings to an end, the jubilant supporters invaded the arena.

Millwall Athletic: Cox, Burgess, Allan, Smith, Goldie, Millar, Dryburgh, Brearley, J.H.Gettins, Banks, Nicol.
Southampton: Robinson, Meehan, Durber, Meston, Chadwick, Petrie, Turner, Yates, Farrell, Wood, Milward.

Millwall Athletic v. Watford

5 January 1907   Southern League
North Greenwich   Attendance: 5,000

Millwall came into this match with just five goals to their name from the nine previous games, which included seven consecutive defeats. But at the end of ninety minutes, the Lions had hit ten goals past their deflated opponents, their best return in this competition since thumping Wolverton 12-0 in 1896. Followers of both teams had eagerly anticipated this game. The visitors won the toss and took advantage of the slight breeze at their backs. It was, however, the home team who were the first to show, with Billy Hunter forcing an early corner that came to nothing. Watford then cleared their lines to set up their initial assault on the goal.

Having repelled this foray, Millwall broke and carried the ball upfield to take the lead in the 5th minute through Hunter, who latched onto a pass from Johnny Blythe and, despite the attentions of Aston the Watford left-back, coolly beat Biggar in the Hornets' goal. Alf Twigg then instigated a round of passing which ended with the prominent Hunter testing the qualities of Biggar, who was relieved to fist the ball out of harm's way.

The 'Flying Scot' wasn't to be denied, however, and it came as no surprise when Millwall increased their lead. Hunter's second came after he had been initially stopped by Aston. The loose ball was retrieved by Twigg, who carried on up the flank and put in a delightful centre. This was well met by Hunter (who had taken up Twigg's position in the middle) to head home goal number two.

This naturally jolted Watford into the attack. Their first real attempt was thwarted by 'Tiny' Joyce's full-length save from Law. The pace of the game quickened, with the half-backs of both sides now dominating – Hitch of Watford catching the eye both in attack and defence.

A further threat to the Millwall goal came when Law beat Fred Shreeve in a run, but once more Joyce was equal to the winger's strike, this time at the expense of a corner. Millwall proceeded to again take up the gauntlet and a fine combination of passes saw Percy Milsom put Alf Dean way down the right. From near the corner flag, he put in an excellent cross for Twigg to apply the finishing touch for Millwall's third.

Straight from the restart, Watford threatened Joyce once again, only for the giant goalkeeper to save once more. Immediately afterwards, his own forwards attacked, the move ending with Dick Jones' shot being blocked by Richardson. Watford's response was a quick counter involving Scottish international Tom Niblo, Foster, and Turner. They reached the Millwall area with some neat passing football, before Lions full-back Stevenson's interception set Jones off on a run which was halted by Aston's tackle on the stroke of half-time.

The second period commenced with a Watford attack that broke down when Millwall gained possession through Dick Jones, although the Welshman's effort was nipped in the bud when Richardson charged his shot down. The Lions excursions into their opponents half were now becoming frequent. As a result of one of them, Twigg took his sides' fourth goal from yet another of Dean's crosses, after Hunter had created the move down the left flank.

Millwall's flowing football had their opponents on the rack. The frustration of the home side's previous form began to evaporate as Millwall attacked at will. The

---

Millwall Athletic 10   **Watford 1**   **Referee:** Mr J. Mason
Hunter (2), Twigg (5),   *Foster*
R. Jones, Milsom (2)

W.B. (Billy) Hunter scored a brace in the 10-1 win against Watford. He scored 15 goals throughout the season having been signed fron Alva Albion Rangers in Scotland. In the 224 games he played between 1904 and 1909 he scored 69 goals.

Alf Twigg scored five goals against Watford to add to his 27 goals that season. He was signed by Millwall from Burton Albion and played 182 games scoring 88 goals between 1905 and 1910.

Millwall: Joyce, Shreeve, Stevenson, Riley, Comrie, Blythe, Dean, Milsom, Twigg, Jones, Hunter.
Watford: Biggar, Richardson, Aston, Main, Hitch, Badger, Soar, Turner, Foster, Niblo, Law.

strain was beginning to show on the Hornets and things got worse for them as George Comrie gained possession and powered forward to set up Jones for claim number five.

At this stage Millwall took their second wind, with Watford enjoying their best spell of the game. The visitors forced Stevenson to clear, and from the resultant throw-in the ball was worked to Foster, who gratefully slipped it past Joyce for what was to be their only telling contribution of the afternoon.

This reverse stirred the Lions to greater efforts, and Twigg duly completed his hat trick with a shot of high velocity that gave the beleaguered Biggar no chance whatsoever, registering the Lions' sixth goal. Watford now pressed forward to add some respectability to the score, and Joyce had to be alert to stop a Foster shot. However, it was the Lions who maintained the attacking momentum, with Jones being very unfortunate in not adding to his tally with another strike on the Watford goal.

Millwall now breached their opponents' rearguard at will, with number seven arriving through Milsom's header via the courtesy of a cross from Hunter. There was no stopping the home team now, with a desolate Watford side waiting for the final whistle. More misery was heaped on them when the persistent Twigg hit number eight with a long-range strike.

The Millwall supporters were becoming frantic at seeing such a goal feast, and when Jimmy Riley broke up another half-hearted Watford raid up he sent Dean away, whose cross was cleared by Richardson at the expense of a corner. Although this came to nothing, Biggar's goal kick only found the lurking Hunter, who immediately released Jones. His run went unchallenged to set up the eighth goal when he unselfishly squared the ball for Twigg to convert an easy tap in.

Suffering Watford fell once more to the same Jones-Twigg combination when the duo set up number nine, the latter hammering home an unstoppable shot to take his personal tally to five. By this time the contest had become Millwall versus Biggar. The hapless goalkeeper was powerless in the face of such onslaught and his team-mates resorted in kicking long and hard up field just for some respite.

Number ten wasn't long in arriving, when Milsom executed the *coup de grâce* to cap one of many fine individual performances when he took a lovely pass to thump the ball past the unsighted Biggar, despite the close attentions of Aston and Richardson.

1906/07:

P	W	D	L	F	A	PTS
38	18	6	14	71	50	42

Southern League First Division
Seventh Place
Manager: George Saunders
Top Goalscorer: Alf Twigg (18)
Average Attendance: 6,579

Millwall football team 1906/07. From left to right: Jones, Brown, Aitken, Hunter, Joyce, Comrie, Stevenson, Twigg, Millar, Blythe, Riley.

Percy Milsom (left) scored two goals against Watford. He played 94 games for Millwall and scored 26 goals between 1905 and 1908. Dick Jones (right) also scored against Watford. He was a Welsh international who came through the junior side at Millwall, St John's. He played 328 games and scored 85 goals between 1899 and 1910.

MILLWALL v. LEYTON

19 April 1909
Boleyn Ground, London

London FA Challenge Cup final
Attendance: 8,000

Millwall returned to the scene of their semi-final triumph in this inaugural knockout competition, having defeated Spurs there 2-1 a month earlier. They had previously beaten the amateurs Ilford 6-0 in the first round and then Chelsea in the second by the odd goal in three.

What made this victory over Leyton all the sweeter was the fact that, for all but five minutes of the second half, the Lions had played a man short as Hector Shand was forced to retire from the fray after picking up a couple of nasty knocks before the interval.

During the opening twenty minutes of this seesaw encounter there had hardly been anything to choose between the two sides, who had put in a fair amount of shots at either end but none that caused any trouble to the goalkeepers. However, after that opening period, it was Millwall who gained the ascendancy with three corner kicks in quick succession that were all cleared.

A rare raid into the Millwall area saw 'Tiny' Joyce foil a hard shot from Kingaby, but Millwall came back and on 35 minutes Alf Twigg, having controlled a pass from Shand, opened the Lions' account by beating Foxcroft in the Leyton goal. Moments later the young triallist Stokes had the opportunity to put Millwall further ahead, but his failure to kill a splendid ball from Jimmy Morris meant the chance was lost.

Further pressure from Millwall kept Leyton under the cosh, with probing from the former England man Dan Cunliffe and the penetrating runs of Morris. It was from one of a spate of corner kicks that Millwall went further ahead when Leyton's inability to clear their lines left Twigg the simple task of tapping his and Millwall's second goal in the 40th minute.

Five minutes after the resumption, outside right Shand limped off the pitch to leave the Lions down to ten men for virtually all of the second half. This turn of events gave Leyton the incentive to batter them for the next quarter of an hour, as Millwall fought to cling on to their two-goal lead.

If the Lions had held all the aces in attack during the first half, it was the

George Comrie played 200 games, scoring 2 goals, between 1905 and 1909.

Millwall 2
Twigg (2)

Leyton 0

Referee: J.R. Schumacher

Millwall team, from left to right, back row: R. Hunter (trainer), Mr J. Beveridge (secretary), S. Frost, A. Archer, J. Joyce, H. Carmichael, J. Jeffrey, A. Sutherland, E. Moor (groundsman), Mr W. Dickinson (director). Middle row: Mr G.A. Saunders (director), H. Shand, D. Cunliffe, J. Blythe, G. Comrie, J. Riley, R. Jones, J. Tellum. Front row: A. Dean, F. Vincent, G. Stevenson, A. Twigg, W.B. Hunter.

defence who now came into their own, especially goalkeeper Joyce, who denied Leyton an early chance to pull a goal back. When Renneville, the Leyton centre forward, missed an open goal, the East London team must have realised it wasn't going to be their day.

After quelling Leyton's onslaught – in which the Millwall backs, Jeffrey and Stevenson, had excelled – the Lions began to pick up the pace once more to threaten their opponents' goal and in doing so play out time. With no further scoring, they finished as worthy winners to become the first holders of a magnificent trophy.

1908/09

P	W	D	L	F	A	PTS
40	16	6	18	59	61	38

Southern League First Division
Eleventh Place
Manager: George Saunders
Top Goalscorer: Fred Vincent (9) Dick Jones (9)
Average Attendance: 6,450

Millwall: Joyce, Jeffrey, Stevenson, Riley, Comrie, Blythe, Shand, Cunliffe, Stokes, Twigg, Morris.

Leyton: Foxcroft, Busby, Longworth, Gray, Morris, Cresser, Phillips, Buchanan, W.T. Renneville, E. Clark, Kingaby.

Millwall v. Portsmouth

8 October 1910 — Southern League
North Greenwich — Attendance: 7,000

After twenty-five years of promoting the game of association football on the Isle of Dogs, the club bade farewell to its roots with a splendid victory over their old adversaries Portsmouth in the last Southern League match the island would see. The directors had come the conclusion some time before, that for Millwall to progress as a club they would have to depart the area that had given birth to the club and seen it grow into a professional organisation.

A moderate crowd assembled to witness this historic occasion, with many fans disillusioned with the move probably deciding not to attend in protest. Skipper Joe Wilson won the toss and elected on the ends. Louch, Pompey's amateur forward, set the game in motion, only for Millwall to take up the early running, with some prolonged possession mainly through the labour of 'Buck' Vincent, who tested Cope with a fine shot. Moments later, the pressure that Millwall had been applying paid off handsomely, when Blythe fed Vincent and in one movement his twenty-yard effort rocketed past Cope to put Millwall one up.

Pompey hit back with a couple of strikes from Kirby, but the Lions were soon on the offensive, with Cope the Portsmouth 'keeper being kept busy with a string of corners, most of which had been conceded by his harassed team-mate Thompson in an effort to keep the ball away from Vincent and his livewire partner Bert Lipsham, who was wreaking havoc down Pompey's right flank whenever he gained possession.

Cope was handling virtually everything thrown at him with great fortitude, but he needed Warner's assistance when a dangerous-looking centre from Lipsham was headed clear, before Vincent put in another great attempt to put Millwall further ahead. Portsmouth's Kirby wasn't having a particularly good day in front of goal as he failed to connect with a couple of chances, and, when he did get his aim right, his shot went straight to Carmichael.

Louch then made a break before being robbed by Jeffrey, who set his team on an attack that resulted in another corner. This was taken by Charlie Elliott, whose cross came to Blythe who put in Johnny Martin to score from close range after 30 minutes (with Portsmouth claiming offside). The remaining quarter of an hour of the first half saw Millwall pound their opponents' goal, and only a fine save from Cope to deny Martin stopped them from falling further behind.

Pompey came out for the second half in a determined mood to reduce the arrears, and it was Carmichael who, after a fairly sedate first forty-five minutes, came into his own with a good save from Louch. At the other end, Martin was pulled up twice for straying offside before Walker hit a screamer that Cope confidently dealt with. However, in an effort to evade the onrushing attackers the Pompey 'keeper took too many steps and was penalised. Quick thinking by Elliott when taking the resulting kick gave Martin the chance to add number three.

Lipsham who was having his best game since joining Millwall from Fulham, was a constant thorn to the Portsmouth defence, although his impact would have been much greater had he been given the ball a lot more.

Millwall began to tire in the last twenty minutes, which was not surprising given the energies that the players had exhausted. It was during this period that Portsmouth

---

Millwall Athletic 3
Vincent
J. Martin (2)

Portsmouth 1
Turner

Referee: Mr J.W. Howcroft

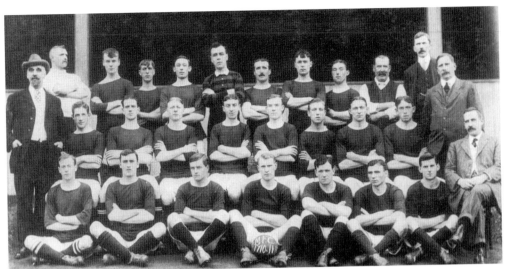

Millwall team 1910-11. From left to right, back row: Mr W. Dickinson, R. Hunter, J. Hawkins, A. Rice, J. Atkinson, H. Carmichael, J. Jeffrey, R. Payne, W. Voisey, E. Moor, Mr J. Beveridge, Mr F.G. Weedon. Middle row: J. Harrower, A. Garrett, S. Frost, J. Wilson, J. Blythe, A. Taylor, S. Wayment, C. Elliot, Mr T. Thorne. Front row: J. Morris, J. Martin, R. Walker, W. Martin, J. Smith, F. Vincent, H.B. Lipsham.

had their best spell and their consolation goal: Noble's fine run ended with Louch nearly scoring, but it was left to Turner to apply the finishing touch with 15 minutes to go.

1910/11:

P	W	D	L	F	A	PTS
38	11	9	18	42	54	31

Southern League First Division
Fifteenth Place
Manager: George Saunders
Top Goalscorer: John Martin (12)
Average Attendance: 11,136

Fred Vincent scored a twenty-yard rocket. The local boy played 207 games scoring 49 goals between 1907 and 1914.

Millwall Athletic: Carmichael, Garrett, Jeffrey, Frost, Wilson, Blythe, Elliott, Walker, J. Martin, Vincent, Lipsham.
Portsmouth: Cope, Thompson, Warner, Yates, Buick, A.E. Knight, Noble, Kirby, L.A. Louch, Turner, A. Turner.

Millwall v. West Ham United

9 March 1912
The Den, London

Southern League
Attendance: 25,000

Eighteen months earlier this encounter would have been a real 'East End' tear up, although Millwall's removal to New Cross had not lessened the local rivalry that existed between the supporters of both clubs. The catalyst of Millwall's emphatic victory was Wally Davis, the Lions centre forward. He had been signed the previous autumn from under the noses of West Ham from the Custom House club who were based deep in Hammer's territory. From the outset, it was the Lions' forward play that gave them the upper hand. Any team, even with the best defence, would have been found wanting in trying to deny a rampant Millwall attack, whose speed and accurate shooting had their visitors on the back foot for most of the game. The ponderous pairing of the Hammers' full-backs, Rothwell and Glover, did not help their cause and they found themselves three down at half time.

West Ham's initial tactic of playing high up the field was a recipe for disaster, as the Lions nippy forwards took full advantage of the space given to them. Charlie Elliott was the first to exploit the weakness in the Hammers' rearguard, which he did after 10 minutes, his long range strike beating Hughes. Fifteen minutes later the hapless 'keeper was picking the ball out of the net once more when Wilson smashed a direct free kick past him from just outside the box.

Just before the interval, Davis decided to get in on the act when, following another Millwall attack, the ball arrived at his feet from a mêlée in font of the West Ham goal. The Welshman gleefully crashed a decisive drive past Hughes to put Millwall firmly in the driving seat.

West Ham commenced the second forty-five minutes with the attitude of making a game of it. They reduced the deficit when Harrison headed home a well-placed corner from Ashton. No sooner had the visitors finished congratulating themselves, however, when the Lions restored the three-goal margin with Davis notching his second after receiving a centre from Wayment.

If the Hammers' defence wasn't exactly covering themselves in glory, their forwards never gave up the ghost, as Joel in the Millwall goal was forced to save two excellent strikes from Harrison and Caldwell. As the referee was about to blow the whistle, Davis capped a fine afternoon's work by netting his hat trick with a shot from close range.

NEXT THURSDAY, Kick-off 3.30 p.m.,

South-Eastern and Chatham Railway v East London Railway.

In aid of RAILWAYMEN'S CONVALESCENT HOME.

KENT LEAGUE CHAMPIONSHIP,

NEXT SATURDAY, Kick-off 3.30 p.m.,

Millwall v. Sheppey Untd.

Millwall Athletic 5
Elliott,
Wilson
Davis (3)

West Ham United 1
Harrison

Referee: T.P. Campbell (Blackburn)

Above: Joe Wilson scored direct from a free kick.

Left: Wally (Wiggy) Davis who scored a hat trick. Although he only turned out 19 times he scored 12 goals and was joint top goalscorer with centre half, Wilson. Davis was signed from Metrugas FC and played 142 games scoring 91 goals between 1911 and 1915. He was also a Welsh international.

This was a terrific result for Millwall, the score line indicating a fairly one-sided affair. It is, however, interesting to note that of the ten corners awarded, seven fell to the Hammers. One thing that is certain is that it was marvellous team effort that won the game, played in front of an attendance of between 25,000-27,000 – a new record for The Den.

1911/12

P	W	D	L	F	A	PTS
38	15	10	13	60	57	40

Southern League First Division
Eighth Place
Manager: Bert Lipsham
Top Goalscorer: Joe Wilson (12) Wally Davis (12)
Average Attendance: 12,631

Millwall Athletic: Joel, Kirkwood, Jeffrey, Martin, Wilson, Liddell, Wayment, Quinn, Davis, Vincent, Elliott.

West Ham United: Hughes, Rothwell, Glover, Redward, Woodards, Blackburn, Ashton, Shea, Harrison, Butcher, Caldwell.

MILLWALL v. SWANSEA TOWN

18 February 1922   FA Cup third round
The Den, London   Attendance: 30,700

The main talk about this game would be the achievement of centre forward Billy Keen. His four-goal salvo was the first by a Millwall player since the club became a member of the Football League. The man of the match, however, was undoubtedly Alf Moule, whose speed in thought as well as in action was the main concern for divisional rivals Swansea Town.

From the start, Millwall set their stall out in a business-like manner. Without overdoing it and with few frills, Moule hogged the ball for most of the game. It soon became apparent that the Welshmen were in for a testing afternoon, and the Lions gained the early reward that their play deserved when Keen scrambled the ball home after 12 minutes.

The masterful Moule was now dictating all aspects of Millwall's forays, and was the fulcrum of all their enterprising football. His long passes to both wings kept the Swans full-backs, Robson and Milne, continually under pressure and it was another probing Moule contribution a minute or so from the interval that sent Dorsett away. His clever run and centre was met by Keen, whose great anticipation and superb connection put the Lions 2-0 up.

The game was now virtually over as a contest, with Millwall and the effervescent Keen obtaining a further two goals in the second half. The Swans had very little to offer in attack to worry the Lions. When they did threaten it was spasmodic, although they nearly scored on a couple of occasions and probably deserved a consolation goal.

Apart from the role of Moule and Keen in this fairly one-sided encounter, Millwall had one of those days when every player was on their game, from the goalkeeper to the outside left, with half-backs Riddell and Voisey maintaining a strong presence throughout, plus the added bonus of young Dick Hill at left-back.

The most encouraging feature was the Lions' forward play, which was undertaken at great pace with the ball control being of the highest order.

1921/22:

P	W	D	L	F	A	PTS
42	10	18	14	38	42	38

Third Division (South)
Twelfth Place
Manager: Bob Hunter
Top Goalscorer: Billy Keen (8)
Average Attendance: 17,523

Millwall 4   Swansea Town 0
  Keen (4)

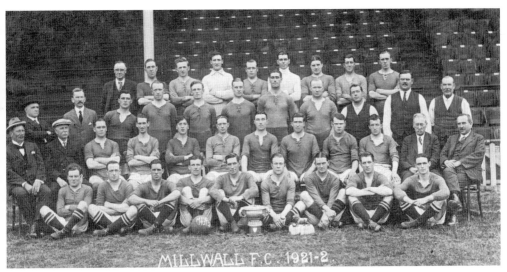

Millwall FC 1921/22. From left to right, back row: A. Gilles (secretary), T. Murray, J. Gallagher, J. Lansdale, J. Fort, F. Wood, R. Thompson, W. Woodley, R. Hill. Third row: R. Hunter (manager), J. Beveridge (director), A. Griffiths, J. Terris, H. Bearton, W. Thomas, A.F. Gomm, R. Duffus, R. Jones (trainer), J. Joyce (assistant trainer), E. Moor (groundsman). Second row: F.G. Weedon (director), G. Saunders (director), G. Taylor, P. Donoghue, T. McGovern, J. Riddell, W. Voisey, W. Stanton, J. Dempsey, C. Sutherland, J.B. Skeggs (director), F. Thorne (chairman). Front row: M. Hopper, S.C. Sayer, A. Moule, W. Keen, J. Richardson, C. Hannaford, J. Walters, J. Dorsett, J. Musgrove.

Billy Keen, the Millwall forward, who had the extraordinary experience of scoring all his side's four goals in the Cup-tie against Swansea.

Millwall: Lansdale, Fort, Hill, Voisey, Riddell, Stanton, Taylor, Moule, Keen, Hannaford, Dorsett.
Swansea Town: Denoon, Robson, Milne, Williams, Collins, Gray, Hoyland, Jones, Edmondson, Brown, Spottiswood.

MILLWALL v. NORWICH CITY

28 August 1926
The Den, London

Football League Third Division (South)
Attendance; 25,000

Bob Parker's five-goal haul is still a Football League record for Millwall, although in 1960/61 Peter Burridge and Joe Broadfoot came very close when they both scored four against Chester and Rochdale respectively. The 1926/27 campaign would be a personal triumph for Bob, who in 40 League appearances hit 37 goals (which is still a record at the club).

This opening day fixture pitted the Lions against the Canaries, and given Millwall's frequent failure in front of goal since the inception of the Third Division, this encounter would turn into a veritable goal feast and a very one-sided affair.

Parker gave Millwall an early lead, his first goal coming from a header that defied all logic, being scored from a seemingly impossible angle. However, Joe Richmond, one of seven players making their City debuts, gave his team some hope when he managed to draw the Canaries level.

Parker restored Millwall's lead just before the break, before Dellow (the amateur striker) claimed Millwall's third. This set the Lions on their way, as Parker decided to make this a one-man show.

It was his deceptive body swerve and pace that was causing the City defence all manner of problems, especially when he was dropping deep to pick up a pass. He received most of these from the hard working Alf Moule, whose ability to give the right ball at the right time continually had the Canaries on the back foot. Bob went on to complete a memorable second half off-the-cuff hat-trick that was described by contemporary reports as 'clever', giving Millwall their biggest opening day victory in the Football League.

1926/27:

P	W	D	L	F	A	PTS
42	23	10	9	89	51	56

Third Division (South)
Third Place
Manager: Bob Hunter
Top Goalscorer: Richard Parker (37)
Average Attendance: 16,047

Richard Parker scored a record 5 goals and was leading scorer with 38 in 1926/27. He signed from Queens Park Rangers and played 106 games scoring 71 goals between 1924 and 1927.

Millwall 6
Parker (5)
R.C. Dellow

Norwich City 1
Richmond

Referee: Mr J.C. O'Neill

Jack Fort (right) and Dick Hill (bottom left), both full-backs and England internationals, were long-serving Lions. Jack signed from Exeter and between 1914 and 1930 played 332 games. Dick signed as an amateur in 1919 and played 392 games between 1919 and 1930.

Millwall: Lansdale, Tilling, Hill, Gomm, W.I. Bryant, F. Martin, Chance, Moule, Parker, R.C. Dellow, Gore.
Norwich City: Dennington, Hannah, Cornwall, Wall, I. Martin, McGrae, Wigg, Cropper, Richmond, Price, Aitken

MILLWALL v. MIDDLESBROUGH

19 February 1927
The Den, London

FA Cup fifth round
Attendance: 44,250

Millwall took full advantage of the early chances that came their way. After 30 minutes play at Cold Blow Lane they were three goals to the good, and seemingly on their way to a comfortable fifth round victory.

It was Lions inside-right Archie Gomm who opened the scoring as early as the third minute by using his long reach to good effect to head past Billy Mathieson in the 'Boro goal from Georgie Chance's cross. Ten minutes later, Mathieson was picking the ball out of the net once again, after a fabulous cross shot from Black put the Lions 2-0 up.

Middlesbrough's response was immediate, and in their first menacing attack they were awarded a penalty kick when Alf Amos was adjudged to have fouled England international George Camsell in the area. It was Camsell himself who took the kick, only to see his effort cannon off the crossbar. Moments later he was further dismayed when his shot smacked against an upright.

Nearly a third of the game had elapsed when Millwall went 3-0 ahead. Outside right Chance took it upon himself to cut inside on a mazy run that left four defenders in his wake, and when confronted by Mathieson he coolly slipped the ball past the advancing 'keeper.

Middlesbrough's woeful luck continued to befall them, with Camsell (again) and Billy Birrell striking Joe Lansdale's timber frame; when they failed to score from the penalty spot for a second time, they must have assumed it was not going to be their day.

After the interval, the pacy Harold Pease made amends for his penalty lapse in the first half by reducing the arrears. 'Boro's neat and tidy build up on their left flank had finally given them some reward. In fact, Pease was fast becoming a thorn in Millwall's side and with about seventeen minutes remaining, his thunderous shot was only partially cleared by the Lions' defence. This left an opportunity for the former Clapton Orient winger Owen Williams to score with yet another cross shot.

Although Middlesbrough scored twice in the second half, it was their forward play in the first period that had really troubled Millwall. Fortunately, the North East side's defensive frailties led to their downfall. Millwall's strength lay in their vastly superior backs, and in the amateur centre-half W.I. ('Billy') Bryant they had the man of the match, who not only found time to keep the marauding Camsell reasonably quiet (he would score 59 goals that season) but also managed to set his own forwards up with magnificent returns. When the final whistle sounded, thousands of Millwall supporters invaded the pitch to raise goalkeeper Lansdale upon their shoulders in appreciation of Joe's contribution to a typical FA Cup tie.

1926/27:

P	W	D	L	F	A	PTS
42	23	10	9	89	51	56

Third Division (South)
Third Place
Manager: Bob Hunter
Top Goalscorer: Richard Parker (37)
Average Attendance: 16,047

Millwall 3
Gomm
Black
Chance

Middlesbrough 2
Pease
O. Williams

Referee: A.E. Fogg (Bolton)

George Chance scored the winner. Signed from Gillingham he played 212 games and scored 33 goals between 1925 and 1930.

Archie Gomm opened the scoring in the first couple of minutes. He was signed from Wycombe Wanderers and played 226 games scoring 20 goals between 1920 and 1931.

Millwall: Lansdale, Fort, Hill, Amos, W.I. Bryant, Graham, Chance, Gomm, Parker, Phillips, Black.
Middlesbrough: Mathieson, Sgt F. Twine, Freeman, Miller, Ferguson, Ashman, Pease, Birrell, Camsell, Carr, O. Williams.

MILLWALL v. TORQUAY UNITED

29 August 1927   Football League Third Division (South)
The Den, London   Attendance: 10,000

1927/28 was to be Millwall's season of destiny in finally gaining promotion. They had finished third in the two previous campaigns, but this one had started with a crushing defeat at Northampton – after holding a 2-1 interval lead, the Lions lost the plot completely in the second half to go down 2-5. This was not what the supporters were expecting.

On the other hand, new boys Torquay United had begun their initial season in the Football League by easing themselves into a new environment with a 1-1 draw the previous Saturday against Devon rivals Exeter City. On their first visit to London, however, United were to face a humiliating experience against a Millwall side that by their own high standards didn't really play that well (and did not really have to).

In fact, the Lions should have had more goals from this game, with the usually reliable Landells being the main culprit. He had definitely left his shooting boots at home, as poor Torquay failed individually as well as a team. Their co-ordination was dreadful and they kicked the ball anywhere and everywhere as Millwall began to take full control.

United's trouble lay in their half-back line, who failed in all aspects of defensive play. Their positional sense was of such wretched proportions that the Lions had the freedom to exploit gaps in the rearguard almost at will. The Torquay forwards, of which little was seen, only came to life briefly during the middle of the second half when Thomson scored their only goal from a corner taken by Mackey. By this stage, Millwall were going through the motions as they game had been won long before.

Another deciding factor in the home team's favour was the speed of all their forwards who, along with Bryant, continued to run riot. It was hardly surprising Torquay crumpled under such pressure, as Millwall raced into a three-goal lead in the first fifteen minutes.

It was Jimmy Hawkins who put the Lions 1-0 up after five minutes when heading home a corner. Two minutes later he followed up a Landells shot that Milsom had made a meal of to score his, and Millwall's, second. It was Milsom again who contributed to third goal when he initially saved a free kick from Phillips, but could not hold the ball. It fell to Landells who had the easy task of tapping into an empty net.

The Lions went further ahead when Phillips scored the best goal of the evening by crashing home a fine drive from thirty-five yards for Millwall to take in a 4-0 lead at the break. The marauding Bill Bryant scored his first of the game seven minutes into the second half, when he was at the end of a swift passing move involving all five forwards.

Hawkins completed his hat trick with number six, before Phillips hit the seventh with another fine drive. After United's consolation, it was left to Billy Bryant to complete his treble, with two well-taken strikes. The first of these came after a mazy run and dribble, while his third goal, and Millwall's ninth, was the product of an accurate shot.

This was the start of a record-breaking season for Millwall, as Coventry City would also feel the icy chill of Cold Blow Lane when they too crumbled to a 9-1 defeat the following November. Poor Torquay made their way back to Devon,

Millwall 9	Torquay United 1	Referee: Mr A.S. King
Hawkins (3),	*Thomson*	
Phillips (2), Bryant (3),		
Landells		

W.I. (Billy) Bryant made his debut at the start of the 1925/26 season when Millwall beat local rivals Crystal Palace. He remained an amateur all of his career. This tall, strapping centre half scored his only Football League hat trick for the Lions in this game. His tally of 30 goals all came in the Football League and when he scored, Millwall never lost.

the home of clotted cream. For this occasion, however, the whipped variety would seem more appropriate!

1927/28:

P	W	D	L	F	A	PTS
42	30	5	7	127	50	65

Third Division (South)
Champions
Manager: Bob Hunter
Leading Goalscorer: John Landells (33)
Average Attendance: 18,095

Millwall: Lansdale, Tilling, Hill, Amos, W.I. Bryant, Graham, Chance, Hawkins, Landells, Phillips, Black.
Torquay United: Milsom, Cook, Smith, Wellock, Wragge, Connor, Mackey, Turner, Jones, McGovern, Thomson.

MILLWALL v. LEYTON

7 May 1928
Boleyn Ground, London

London FA Challenge Cup Final
Attendance: 8,000

This final was a repeat of the 1909 version, when the same two clubs had met to contest the first such event in this competition. It was the Lions' fourth London Cup final: of the previous three they had won two (1909 and 1914) and had been runners-up once (1912).

When Millwall's famous amateur Billy Bryant won the toss against his fellow non-professional colleagues, he elected to take advantage of the prevailing wind. From the start the Lions had their opponents under very heavy pressure, as three early corner kicks testified. With Leyton's first attack petering out through Dick Hill's intervention, Millwall went upfield to score after 6 minutes.

It was the irrepressible Jack Cock who opened his side's account, when Burr (who had already denied Landells with a sensational left-handed save), was bundled over the line with the ball after he had collected a centre from George Chance. The amateurs' response was swift through the enterprise of Lockwood. He went on a solo run with his final shot going in off Harford's upright.

Following this, man-of-the-moment Jack Cock scored in the 14th, and 15th minutes to complete a nine-minute hat-trick. The first was a close range effort, after receiving a pass from Wilf Phillips; the second arrived when he put the finishing touch to a goalmouth scramble. Leyton now had the almost impossible task of retrieving anything but pride from the game.

Still Millwall continued to monopolise the proceedings. The match was turning in a rout, with the Lions seeming to score at will. A further two shots entered the Leyton net before the half hour had been reached: Cock in the 23rd minute with number four, while two minutes later Phillips got in on the act by slotting home number five.

Incredibly, Leyton refused to throw in the towel. They were duly rewarded for this approach after 28 minutes had elapsed, when Hall won his tussle with Lions full-back Jack Fort to prod the ball to Lockwood, who forced it home. This tweaking of the Lions' tail spurred them forward and it was Burr who gained the applause of the crowd when dealing very effectively with Cock's hard low drive.

The second half started very much like the first with Black forcing a corner, from which Chance placed his shot wide of the target. But it was the amateurs who were now showing much more coordination in their play, which resulted in a corner being awarded for Dellow's persistence, after fine approach work by Hawkings and Smith.

Play was moving nicely from end to end, with Fort and Alf Amos combining to clear another Leyton corner, which was followed by a Dellow long-range shot that caused Harford no trouble at all. Burr was called upon once more when punching away from Landells, which gave Cock, the chance to add to his tally – but his shot screamed inches over the bar.

Leyton were more than holding their own in this period, and it was they who opened the scoring of this half, when in the 59th minute Smith received a pass from the excellent Dellow (who had previously played in Millwall's first team) to deceive Harford with a fine shot. Moments later, the 'keeper had difficulty in dealing with Lockwood's curling centre, but managed to get a fist on the ball to clear his lines.

Having taken their foot off the gas, the Lions found it hard to regain their

---

Millwall 6
Cock (4)
Phillips,
Landells

Leyton 3
Lockwood
Smith
Dellow

Referee: H.E. Grey

Millwall FC Third Division League Champions 1927/28. From left to right, back row: A.H. Amos, J. Fort, G.B. Harford, R.H. Hill, L. Graham. Front row: G.H. Chance, J. Landells, J.G. Cock, W.J. Phillips, A.G. Black, W.F. Bryant.

momentum, and another Leyton goal looked on the cards. After Smith had shot narrowly over, it came about when a pass from Hall rebounded off his team-mate Hawkings into the path of Dellow, who gave Harford no chance with a first-time drive into the bottom left-hand corner with a quarter of an hour to play.

This minor setback gave Millwall their second wind and they were able to cash in on a flagging Leyton team who had given their all. Following a free kick in the 80th minute, John Landells brought their score to a round half dozen with the last goal of the game.

1927/28:

P	W	D	L	F	A	PTS
42	30	5	7	127	50	65

Third Division (South)
Champions
Manager: Bob Hunter
Top Goalscorer: John Landells (33)
Average Attendance: 18,095

Millwall: Harford, Fort, Hill, Amos, W.I. Bryant, Collins, Chance, Landells, Cock, Phillips, Black.
Leyton: J.H. Burr, J. Preston, H. Terris, H. Graves, T. Cable, W. Margetts, F. Lockwood, H. Hall, R. Dellow, G. Smith, T.W. Hawkings.

MILLWALL v. CORINTHIANS

20 January 1930
Stamford Bridge, London

FA Cup third round (second replay)
Attendance: 58,775

This was an amazing tie, particularly as both these teams had already played 210 minutes of football without deciding it, and in light of the fact that this match was contested on a Monday afternoon in front of a mammoth crowd of nearly 59,000 (which took the aggregate of paying spectators watching the three games to an incredible 136,000).

No doubt the allure of the cup and the presence of the darlings of the establishment – and amateurs to boot – the renowned Corinthians helped to swell the crowd, but unlike in the first replay at The Den, it was Millwall who drew first blood when after half an hour of play Jack Cock's pass caused panic in the Corinthian defence. Jimmy Forsyth received the ball some twenty-five yards out and seemed to mishit his shot – which deceived the advancing Baker so much that he failed to react, only for the ball to creep into the net.

Taken aback by this unfortunate turn of events, the amateurs drew level before half-time with probably the best goal of the game. A spectacular piece of football came when they were awarded a corner that Robins took, with Ashton touching it on for Graham Doggart who, with his back to goal, performed an overhead kick that gave Bill Wilson in the Millwall goal no chance. The astonishing thing about this effort was that the ball had not touched the ground since the set piece was taken.

After another forty-five minutes of toil there was still nothing to separate the teams, although if there was a factor that was going to favour the Lions it would be that the Corinthians, as amateurs, might begin to feel the effects of three hard ties. The next goal was vital, and whoever scored it seemed likely to go on to win. This theory was tested in the 53rd minute when Billy Corkindale restored Millwall's lead after a short corner had been played him and his acute angled shot found the net, Baker in the Corinthian goal failing to readjust his position in time.

There was an element of good fortune about the Lions' next goal when again Baker was at fault, allowing Millwall's outside left Harry Wadsworth's soft shot to slip from his grasp. His full-back Knight's attempted clearance struck the onrushing Jack Cock, who claimed the third goal for the Lions. It appeared that the Corinthians had given up their resolve for another season. Injuries to their ranks, including Robins, added to their trouble.

It was the former England striker Cock who added a fourth with a long and clever individual effort. Following this, the fine Corinthian spirit and resistance was finally broken when Corkindale, receiving the ball unmarked in front of the goal, had time to trap it and coolly sidefoot it home for his side's fifth and his second goal of the game.

So this saga had eventually come to its conclusion, but it hardly gave Millwall any time to prepare for the fourth round tie against Doncaster Rovers – which was to take place the following Saturday.

Millwall 5
Forsyth,
Corkindale (2)
Cock (2)

Corinthians 1
Doggart

Referee: H.H. Heath (Sheffield)

F.A. CUP THIRD ROUND REPLAY. MILLWALL v. CORINTHIAN. WEDNESDAY, JAN. 15th, 1930.

FOOTBALL LEAGUE—Division 2. Goals

	P	W	L	D	F	A	Pts
Oldham Athletic	...24	15	3	6	59	27	36
Blackpool	...24	17	5	2	65	40	36
Chelsea	...24	11	5	8	43	24	30
Bradford	...24	11	7	6	48	42	28
Bury	...24	12	9	3	49	41	27
Cardiff City	...25	11	9	5	36	35	27
Wolverhampton Wand.	...25	11	9	5	50	46	27
Southampton	...24	11	9	4	51	47	26
Charlton Athletic	...24	9	7	8	37	32	26
Notts Forest	...24	8	8	8	32	38	24
West Bromwich Albion	...24	10	10	4	63	50	24
Hull City	...24	9	10	5	34	42	23
Stoke City	...25	8	11	6	43	47	22
Bradford City	...24	7	10	7	36	44	21
Bristol City	...24	8	11	5	42	53	21
Preston North End	.24	8	11	5	37	48	21
Tottenham Hotspur	...24	7	10	7	29	38	21
Notts County	...25	4	9	12	31	41	20
Millwall	...24	5	10	9	38	54	19
Reading	...24	5	11	8	27	39	18
Barnsley	...24	6	12	6	30	43	18
Swansea Town	...24	6	13	5	32	41	17

SATURDAY, JAN. 18th, at 2 45 p.m.

FOOTBALL LEAGUE

CHELSEA

MONDAY, JAN. 20th, at 2.45 p.m.

SOUTHERN LEAGUE

Grays Thurrock

H. & H. G. Peterken, Printers (T.U.), 158 High St., Poplar, E.14, & at Limehouse and Canning Town Tel.—Bow t365!

1929/30:

P	W	D	L	F	A	PTS
42	12	15	15	57	73	39

Second Division
Fourteenth Place
Manager: Bob Hunter
Top Goalscorer: Jack Cock (15)
Average Attendance: 20,761

Millwall: Wilson, Tyler, Pipe, Martin, Gomm, Graham, Corkindale, Hawkins, Cock, Forsyth, Wadsworth.
Corinthians: B. Howard-Baker, A.G. Bower, J.G. Knight, A.H. Chadder, W.T. Whewell, F.H. Ewer, R.W.V. Robins, T.N.S. Creek, C.T. Ashton, A.G. Doggart, W.S. Parker.

MILLWALL v. CORINTHIANS

Left: Chisel Forsyth scored the first goal in this match against the Corinthians. He also scored the first in the 2-2 draw at the Den. He was signed by Millwall from Gillingham and he played 350 games scoring 49 goals between 1929 and 1939.

Below: From left to right, back row: J. Pipe, W. Wilson, L. Smith. Front row: F. Martin, S. Sweetman, L. Graham.

Jack Cock was a prolific goal scorer for all his clubs. He later became manager in the 1940s signed from Plymouth. He played 135 games and scored 92 goals between 1927 and 1931.

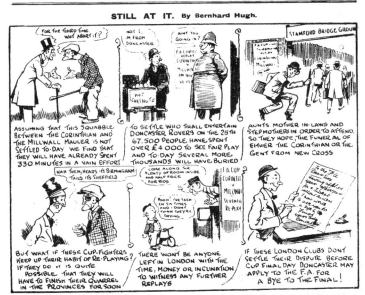

Doncaster wants to know if there is a limit to replays.

MILLWALL v. CHARLTON ATHLETIC

3 January 1931
The Den, London

Football League Third Division (South)
Attendance: 25,000

There was no doubt about this being Millwall's best performance of the season, and to come against local rivals Charlton was all the better to savour. This result still remains the Lions' biggest victory over the Robins – although the margin of the victory did not really do justice to Charlton's contribution to an excellent match in which they had the majority of possession and didn't really utilise it to their advantage.

Considering it was a local derby, the game was played in a very sporting spirit, with just nine stoppages. No one present could have expected what was to come after Andy Swallow had given the Lions a 1-0 lead at the interval (after fine work by Jimmy Poxton and John Readman), at which time the visitors could count themselves a little unfortunate at being a goal down.

Charlton's methodical approach up until the area was of the highest order, but when push came to shove it was Millwall who showed their neighbours how to finish with clinical efficiency. The Lions forwards, led by Johnny Landells, laid siege to the Charlton goal as attack upon attack increased the pressure as the second half got underway.

Taking charge of proceedings, Millwall made their opponents pay for their poor shooting in the first forty-five minutes. The Robins defence began to crack under strain as gaps appeared in their ranks and Millwall took the necessary steps to exploit them. With five minutes of the second half gone, Millwall increased their lead when Landells finished off a move from another precise Poxton cross.

To their credit, Charlton came back into the game, with attacks initiated mainly through Astley and McKay as they applied some extensive pressure and kept the Lions' defenders on their toes. However, Pipe and Sweetman steadied the Millwall boat and – aided and abetted by Charlton's woeful finishing – the home goal remained intact.

It was during this spell that the Charlton halves effected their influence on the game with some crisp tackling and thoughtful passing, but try as they might the Reds just could not breach the Lions' defence, and when they did they found Yuill in outstanding form.

Weathering the storm, Millwall poured forward and were rewarded with two goals in a minute that ended Charlton's resistance, just past the hour mark. It was Readman who leapt to head another cross from the indomitable Poxton, and in the 63rd minute the equally impressive Landells retrieved the ball out on the left wing, cut in past a defender to deliver a pinpoint centre for Wadsworth to gleefully bag number four.

These two goals set the seal on Millwall's dominance as they weaved their way downfield, sweeping aside a very sad looking Charlton defence with ease. There were two more goals for the Lions from Wadsworth and Readman (who both netted a brace), against opponents who were down on their knees at the end.

All of the Millwall goals were the result of well worked and finely finished moves as Millwall's quick thinking and speedy forward line made the Charlton backs, Smith and Langford, look very ponderous, with Swallow playing just his sixth game of the season. However, it was the display of Poxton, and Landells (recently back from injury) who took the honours for Lions with slick build-up play, and excellent use of the ball.

Millwall 6
Swallow, Landells
Readman (2)
Wadsworth (2)

Charlton Athletic 0

Referee: H. Thomas (Walsall)

Football League (Div. 2).   MILLWALL v. CHARLTON.   Saturday, Jan. 3rd, 1931.

FOOTBALL LEAGUE.—Division 2.

	P.	W.	L.	D.	F.	A.	Pts.
Everton	23	16	3	4	73	36	36
West Bromwich Albion	23	13	5	5	50	25	31
Tottenham Hotspur	23	14	7	2	58	29	30
Wolverhampton Wans.	23	15	8	0	57	35	30
Preston North End	23	12	7	4	56	34	28
Burnley	23	11	7	5	49	45	27
Bradford	23	11	8	4	61	39	26
Southampton	23	10	8	5	35	29	25
Bury	23	11	9	3	49	45	25
Port Vale	21	11	9	3	44	41	25
Stoke City	23	9	8	6	35	40	24
Oldham Athletic	24	9	11	4	34	45	22
Swansea Town	23	8	10	5	35	42	21
Charlton Athletic	23	8	10	5	35	45	21
Plymouth Argyle	23	8	12	3	38	49	19
Bristol City	23	7	11	5	29	51	19
Bradford City	23	6	11	6	32	43	18
Barnsley	23	6	11	6	24	44	18
Millwall	23	7	13	3	43	54	17
Notts Forest	23	4	11	8	41	57	16
Cardiff City	23	6	11	4	35	53	16
Reading	24	5	15	4	32	61	14

THE SCORING BOARD.

The letter in the Programme corresponds with the letter on the Board—thus **A 0 1** means that the first-named Club has scored 0 and their opponents 1.

	HOME CLUB	Half-time		AWAY CLUB.	Half-time
A	Bradford City		v.	Barnsley	
B	Burnley		v.	Southampton	
C	Notts Forest		v.	Bradford	
D	Oldham Athletic		v.	Stoke City	
E	Plymouth Argyle		v.	Bury	
F	Port Vale		v.	Bristol City	
G	Preston North End		v.	Reading	
H	Swansea		v.	Everton	
J	Tottenham Hotspur		v.	Wolverhampton Wdrs	
K	West Bromwich		v.	Cardiff City	
L	Leeds United		v.	Arsenal	
M	Manchester United		v.	Chelsea	
N	West Ham Utd		v.	Aston Villa	
P	Fulham		v.	Notts County	
R	Charlton Athletic Reserves		v.	Millwall Reserves	

SATURDAY, JAN. 10th, at 2.45 p.m.

LONDON FOOTBALL COMBINATION.

Crystal Palace Res.

SATURDAY, JAN. 17th, at 2.45 p.m.

FOOTBALL LEAGUE

Oldham Athletic

H. & H. G. Peterken, Printers (T.U.), 15, Bly's St., Poplar, E.1., & at Limehouse and Canning Town. Tel.—East 3358

1930/31:

P	W	D	L	F	A	PTS
42	16	7	19	71	80	39

Second Division
Fourteenth Place
Manager: Bob Hunter
Top Goalscorer: Jack Cock (15)
Average Attendance: 16,142

Harry Wadsworth scored two goals against Charlton. He was signed from Nottingham Forest via Liverpool. He played 85 games scoring 12 goals between 1928 and 1931.

Millwall: Yuill, Sweetman, Pipe, Newcomb, Hancock, Graham, Wadsworth, Readman, Landells, Swallow, Poxton

Charlton Athletic: Robertson, Smith, Langford, Morgan, Millson, Pugsley, Wyper, McKay, Lennox, Astley, Horton.

MILLWALL v. MANCHESTER UNITED

5 May 1934
The Den, London

Football League Second Division
Attendance: 35,000

The far-reaching effects of this game wouldn't be appreciated until many years later. As one United historian has stated, the events of that springtime afternoon in a corner of New Cross known as The Den, saw the seeds sewn in the resurrection of a mere football team into what has become nearly seventy years later a financial institution that has won every award that domestic and European football has thrown at them.

In the short term, United were financially strapped: defeat and relegation would undoubtedly have been disastrous for them, but on the other hand all Millwall required was a point – having gained a draw at Old Trafford earlier in the season. The Lions were expected to get the result they required from the game, although the matter of scoring goals was a concern, having hit just 39 in the previous 41 matches.

A packed Cold Blow Lane, which included a fair number of Mancunians in the crowd to support their favourites, saw referee Mr Whittle of Worcester get the game underway. Considering what was at stake, the match began in a very positive manner with Millwall, roared on by an enthusiastic crowd, setting up an early attack with Laurie Fishlock breaking down the wing to put in a beautiful ball that was meant for the head of Jimmy Yardley, although it was United's 'keeper Jack Hacking's excellent leap that claimed the ball.

Hacking's clearance found his outside-left, Tommy Manley, who made tracks down the flank, and was threatening the Millwall the goal until a marvellous tackle from Lions full-back Jimmy Walsh averted the danger. This action would set the tone for the next twenty-five minutes, during which time another of United's international players, inside left Ernie Hine was injured, being forced to operate on the wing with Manley moving inside.

This setback seemed to galvanise the Mancunians, and with ten minutes of play left before half-time, they got the crucial breakthrough that both teams had been vying for, with a rare chance that opened up for Manley to bang the ball past Yuill in the Millwall goal. Millwall could count themselves unfortunate that the Manchester club held the upper hand at the interval through a sheer piece of opportunism.

Millwall came out for the second half duly fired up and determined to get the goal they required to secure their future in the Second Division. They attacked and attacked but nothing seemed to fall their way, and with the veteran Hacking in splendid form the minutes were ticking by. The Lions fans became anxious, urging their favourites to shoot on sight instead of passing. It was to no avail, however, and it was hard to see where that elusive goal would come from.

Another goal did arrive, but it was the clincher for United. It came about when converted wing-half Hugh McLenahan, pressed into an emergency inside right role, received the ball around the halfway line and made rapid progress towards Millwall's goal before spotting his team mate Jackie Cape making headway down the right.

Putting the winger away with a terrific pass Cape took the ball in his stride, and within a couple of paces unleashed a shot that gave poor Duncan Yuill no chance

Millwall 0	Manchester United 2	Referee: Mr Whittle (Worcester)
	Manley	
	Cape	

End of an era. Len Graham played from 1923 to 1934. This was the last season for Len who spent his entire career with Millwall. He tried to make a comeback against Nottingham Forest in October 1933 after an injury. He played 362 games for Millwall scoring 8 goals. Len's calming presence in the team was sorely missed, and was almost certainly one of the causes of Millwall's relegation in 1934.

whatsoever. With the trap door firmly open, Millwall kept pressing to the bitter end but they just could not find any way past the immaculate Hacking.

So, the Lions were left licking their wounds and facing another spell in the Third Division. United were back in the top flight by 1935, but it took Millwall another four years to reclaim their place in the Second Division, and it would be forty-one years before this pair would meet again in the Football League.

1933/34:

P	W	D	L	F	A	PTS
42	11	11	20	39	68	33

Second Division
Twenty-first Place
Manager: Bill McCracken
Top Goalscorer: Laurie Fishlock (7)
Average Attendance: 19,000

Millwall: Yuill, Walsh, Pipe, Newcomb, Turnbull, Forsyth, McCartney, Alexander, Yardley, Roberts, Fishlock.
Manchester United: Hacking, Griffiths, Jones, Robertson, Vose, McKay, Cape, McLenahan, Ball, Hine, Manley.

Millwall v. Gateshead

12 December 1936
The Den, London

FA Cup second round
Attendance: 18,550

Millwall's advance into the third round was achieved with their highest win in the competition since they became members of the Football League in 1920, coming against a team struggling in the Third Division (North). The Lions were at the top of their form and gave a lively display of bright, fast and entertaining football that gave the Northerners' overworked defence a grilling from start to finish. Gateshead, by contrast, were sluggish in their movements and their failure to take up positions to give and receive passes were made to look very pedestrian by a fluid Millwall team.

Another failing of Gateshead was the habit they displayed of trying to gain an extra yard of space to enable them to get a shot away unimpeded. This was folly from the start, especially with a nimble pair of backs like Tommy Inns and Ted Smith in attendance, whose crisp tackling was of the highest calibre.

With the control of the game firmly in Millwall's grip the Lions' wide players, outside-right Bob Thomas and his colleague on the left Jack Thorogood, rarely wasted a ball. Together with the sterling support of their inside men, it was a surprise that Askew in the Gateshead goal wasn't beaten by more than the seven goals he conceded.

The first arrived after 12 minutes when Thomas, getting the better of his marker, delivered a pinpoint cross for Dave Mangnall to head home. Number two came not long afterwards when Ken Burditt rounded Conroy, only for Thorogood to steal possession and put in a splendid shot which found the far corner of the net. Gateshead were now on the back foot, and poor Askew had shots raining down on him from all angles, and distances. During the course of the match his woodwork was rattled on three occasions, but despite all his bravery, another two goals by Jim McCartney, and Burditt – both taken with sublime skill – entered his net before the interval.

To say the visitors had a mountain to climb would be an understatement, the ease in which Millwall penetrated the visitor's rearguard, both down the middle and on the flanks, made the Lions hungry and ruthless in their pursuit for glory. A Thomas penalty plus further strikes from McCartney and Burditt added more discomfort to Gateshead's porous and dispirited defence. As one can imagine, very little was seen of the Gateshead attack, and to sum up their pitiful day, with the game nearly at its conclusion, and after the Lions had scored their seventh, they did manage a shot to trouble Yuill the Lions 'keeper – although it went straight to him.

Besides the Lions' excellent football the other feature to stand out in this amazing performance was the spectacular nature of all the goals (with the possible exception of the Thomas penalty) which were shared by all the forwards.

1936/37:

P	W	D	L	F	A	PTS
42	18	10	14	64	54	46

Third Division (South)
Eighth Place
Manager: Charlie Hewitt
Top Goalscorer: Ken Burditt (17)
Average Attendance: 19,299

Millwall 7
Mangnall, Thorogood
McCartney, Burditt (3)
Thomas (pen)

Gateshead 0

Referee: Mr P. Snape (Swinton)

Ken Burditt scored a hat-trick. He signed for Millwall from Nottingham Forrest. He played 69 games scoring 34 goals between 1936 and 1938.

Jim McCartney got on the scoresheet.

Bob Thomas scored from a penalty. He joined Millwall from Barnsley and played 13 games scoring 4 goals between 1936 and 1938.

Jack Thorogood shot into the far corner of the net. He joined Millwall from Birmingham and played 88 games scoring 32 goals between 1934 and 1939.

Millwall: Yuill, Smith E, Inns, Brolly, Hancock, Forsyth, Thomas, Mangnall, K. Burditt, McCartney, Thorogood.
Gateshead: Askew, Conroy, Livingstone, Neilson, Inskip, Mathieson, Walker, Heslop, Reed, Oxley, Reay.

MILLWALL v. DERBY COUNTY

20 February 1937
The Den, London

FA Cup fifth round
Attendance: 48,762

Three significant events arose out this Millwall victory. The first was that the Lions avenged the 1903 semi-final defeat at the hands of County, the second was that it set an all-time ground record attendance at The Den, and the third was they came from a goal down to beat a team that would finish in fourth place in that season's First Division campaign.

If Millwall had been apprehensive before the game it didn't show as they more than held their own in the opening ten minutes. Four minutes later, however, disaster struck when, totally against the run of play, County took the lead. They say that lightening doesn't strike twice in the same place – try telling the older Millwall supporters at the game as Keen, the Rams left half, hoisted a free kick into the area from some 35 yards out on the touchline. As the ball sailed into the area it appeared that every player froze – even Burke the unsighted Lions 'keeper who allowed it to drop into the net unassisted. It was extremely reminiscent of Warren's effort at Villa Park some thirty-four years earlier.

Millwall's riposte was instantaneous – and a goal to be proud of. Tom Brolly played a splendid ball into the feet of Dave Mangnall who, as he was about to be tackled, cracked an unstoppable shot form the edge of the box past the despairing Scattergood.

From left to right: Burke, E. Smith, K. Burditt, Wallbanks, Barker, Forsyth, Mangnall, Brolly, McCartney, Daniels, Thorogood.

Millwall 2
Mangnall
McCartney

Derby County 1
Keen

Referee: Mr E.R. Westwood (Walsall)

Derby were rattled into giving away plenty of free-kicks in an effort to stop the Lions making further inroads into their territory, and were undoubtedly thankful when the whistle went for half-time. Millwall started the next forty-five minutes like a team possessed. In the second half Barker – Derby's normally sound centre-half – was prone to many mistakes, but Scattergood stopped his side from falling behind with two excellent saves in quick succession.

Continuing the onslaught a lovely centre from Thorogood was wasted when no other Millwall attacker was at hand to put the Lions into a deserved lead. Dai Astley, County's Welsh international, threatened with his excellent dribbling skills but he rarely made it into the danger areas and when he did Jimmy Wallbanks superbly marshalled him out of harm's way.

A County attack was instigated by Duncan, who swung over a decent cross only for Astley – a yard or so from goal – to head straight to Burke, who eventually cleared upfield, then Napier unluckily hit a Millwall post, before the home team responded in the manner that had gone before, with fight and speed, and finally gained their reward in the 85th minute when McCartney smashed home a glorious volley from twenty yards to give the Lions the spoils of victory.

Dave Mangnall (left) scored yet again in the Cup. A native of Wigan in Lancashire he was signed from West Ham United and played 72 games scoring 48 goals between 1936 and 1938. Jim McCartney (right) got the winner with a volley from 20 yards. He joined Millwall as an outside left from Swindon Town via Newcastle United. He played 184 games between 1933 and 1938 scoring 38 goals.

Millwall: Burke, E. Smith, Inns, Brolly, Wallbanks, Forsyth, Daniels, Mangnall, Burditt, McCartney, Thorogood.
Derby County: Scattergood, Bell, Howe, Nicholas, Barker, Keen, Crooks, Stockill, Astley, Napier, Duncan.

MILLWALL v. DERBY COUNTY

GATE - CRASHERS at the Millwall ground to see Derby County beaten in the Cup-tie yesterday. They wanted grandstand seats.

The photographs above depict the chaotic scenes when the record attendance was set at The Den for the intriguing Cup tie against Derby County.

THE ILLUSTRATED SPORTING AND DRAMATIC NEWS

ROUND FIVE

Millwall beat Derby County at the Den

Action shots taken after the derby game got underway. *Top:* The Derby 'keeper is beaten by Dave Mangnall's opener. *Below:* Jack Thorogood (left) and Ken Burditt try to force the ball home.

MILLWALL v. MANCHESTER CITY

6 March 1937
The Den, London

FA Cup sixth round
Attendance: 42,474

As a result of this historic win Millwall became the first club from the Third Division to reach the semi-final of the FA Cup, and it was the brace from Lancashire-born Dave Mangnall that put mighty Manchester City to the sword, making them the third club from the top division to fall in Millwall's citadel, The Den.

Like the other ties the Lions contested that season, they won in a convincing style, and as early as the 15th minute there was little doubt as to what the outcome of the game would be. On a slippery surface many thought that Millwall's run would come to an end against a City side containing a chock-full of internationals and who were First Division Champions elect.

City started the game, and in the opening moments both sides were passing the ball around before Millwall got into their stride with their customary breakneck pace. Playing some good football, at times they threatened to overrun a City defence that included one of their England players, Sam Barkas, and the equally experienced centre-half, Marshall. It was during this early period that Mangnall gave City some indication of what was to come as he thundered a shot against a post from an acute angle.

Manchester then came on the attack with a good bout of passing that nearly let in Peter Doherty, before they lost wing-half Rogers with a cut eye. It was during his ten-minute absence that the Lions obtained their first goal. Ken Burditt took a corner in which City's blocking of two goalbound efforts was followed by another Millwall corner. Burditt was again the supplier, and on this occasion Mangnall leapt up to thump his header past Frank Swift.

Millwall, like the lion on their shirts, were rampant. A further succession of corners were causing City a fair amount of trouble, and the giant Swift had to make some very good saves to prevent his team falling further behind. With half-time approaching, however, City nearly equalised when Wallbanks blocked Toseland's shot, and then Burke had to be alert to a long-range effort from Bray.

Restarting the game, Millwall continued in the same style as they had for the first forty-five minutes by going on the attack, and after 57 minutes Mangnall claimed his and the Lions' second with another header, this time from McCartney's accurate centre. City then had their best spell of the match in which Alec Herd crashed his shot against Millwall's crossbar, with the ball rebounding down behind Burke but not over the line. If Dave Mangnall had been the Lions' hero with his here-there-and-everywhere display in the attack, then goalkeeper Johnny Burke would play his role in the latter stages when, having emerged with the ball after a scramble on the goal line, the gallant Irishman surpassed himself by stopping a pile-driver from City's outside left Eric Brook.

When the referee blew the final whistle hundreds of fans ran on to the pitch and carried Mangnall in triumph back to the dressing room. Before this game City had harboured ambitions of a Cup and League double – which would have been the first of the twentieth century and that would in actual fact take another twenty-four years before a team accomplished it.

Millwall, needing a point to gain promotion, were backed by a vast following of fans who helped swell a large crowd crammed into the Devon club's homely little ground.

Millwall 2
Mangnall (2)

Manchester City 0

Referee: Mr J.M. Wiltshire
(Sherborne, Dorset)

J. Daniels   J. Thorogood   E. Smith   T. Inns

A good-luck handshake from Mr. Charles Hewitt, and Dave Mangnall leads
the team on to the field for the game against Manchester City. Also in the
picture can be seen J. McCartney (right) and T. Inns (centre)

J. R. Smith   T. Brolly   D. Barker   J. Forsyth

Millwall: Burke, E. Smith, Inns, Brolly, Wallbanks, Forsyth, Burditt, Barker, Mangnall, McCartney,
J.R. Smith.
Manchester City: Swift, Dale, Barkas, Rogers, Marshall, Bray, Toseland, Herd, Tilson, Doherty,
Brook.

MILLWALL v. MANCHESTER CITY

The crowd spills on to the pitch at the Den after the Manchester City Cup game.

Millwall hope to rise to greater heights even than Reg Smith who clears colleagues Wallbanks, E. Smith, K. Burditt and Thorogood in style at The Den.

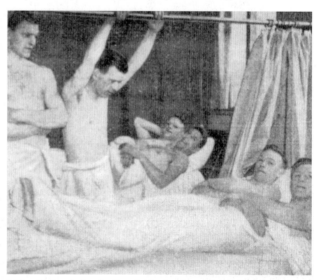

Millwall, Sunderland's Cup rivals, were promised a holiday by the sea if they defeated Manchester City. Here you see some of them at Blackpool enjoying a rest after a bath.

Manchester City's goalkeeper is seen in a vain attempt to save the first goal.

This photograph of Dave Mangnall's first goal against City also shows the magnificent clock on the North Terrace which displays the actual goal time.

EXETER CITY v. MILLWALL

7 May 1938
St James' Park, Exeter

Third Division (South)
Attendance: 13,000

Missing from the Lions line-up was leading scorer Dave Mangnall, sidelined since March with an reoccurring injury, but they still had plenty of attacking options available, and the supporters were in high spirits as the teams kicked off.

Their enthusiasm was severely knocked when Ebdon, the City inside left, scored after three minutes when he slammed home a loose ball, and the passage of play over the next twenty minutes or so were dictated solely by Exeter. The signs were ominous, as nerves got the better of Millwall until Syd Rawlings eased them considerably when, after 25 minutes, he managed to elude his marker to put in a centre that was converted by centre forward John McLeod.

Seven minutes later this same combination set up the move that put the Lions into the lead, but on this occasion the roles were reversed as Rawlings took McLeod's pass to beat Church in the City goal. Exeter, who up to this point had matched Millwall for pace and aggression, could count themselves a little unfortunate going in 2-1 down at half-time.

The second forty-five minutes would be a vastly different proposition. No doubt given some words of encouragement in the interval, Millwall exuded a brand of confidence that saw them sweep their passes, long and short, with accuracy into wide positions that had the City defence reeling as the quality of Millwall's play began to show with Rawlings playing the leading role.

It came as no surprise when the Lions went further in front. Rawlings who was giving Clarke and Angus a torrid time down the flank, centred once again to give McLeod an easy tap in for number three. Not to be outdone, he reacted first to a Jimmy Forsyth free-kick to head home the fourth, as the Lions began to pull away.

The superb Rawlings capped a fine personal display when he claimed his hat-trick after another devastating Millwall move. This gave the Lions a four-goal margin, although in the last quarter of the game City had given as good as they got, and if either or both of Coulston's efforts had gone in and not struck the woodwork (with Yuill beaten) the outcome might have been different.

As the final whistle went, hundreds of jubilant Millwall supporters rushed onto the pitch to hail their heroes, and to carry the buoyant man of the match Syd Rawlings off on their sturdy shoulders. News of Millwall's success down in the West Country was relayed back to The Den, where an incredible crowd of 17,000 were being given regular updates of the happenings at St James' Park while they watched a reserve team fixture.

1937/38:

P	W	D	L	F	A	PTS
42	23	10	9	83	37	56

Third Division (South)
First Place
Manager: Charlie Hewitt
Top Goalscorer: Dave Mangnall (16)
Average Attendance: 22,858

Exeter City 1
Ebdon

Millwall 5
McLeod (2)
Rawlings (3)

Referee: Unknown

Millwall supporters chair Rawlings who just scored a hat-trick in a 5-1 win in the last game of the season to make the Lions Third Division (South) 'Champions'.

A golf day out for the 1937/38 Champions. From left to right: J. McLeod, K.Burditt, J.Thorogood, F.Hedley, G. Burditt, D. Mangnall, E. Steele.

Exeter City: Church, Brown, B. Clarke, Shadwell, Bamsey, Angus, Coulston, Bussey, Bowl, Ebdon, McGill.
Millwall: Yuill, E. Smith, Inns, Brolly, Chiverton, Forsyth, Rawlings, Richardson, McLeod, Barker, J.R. Smith.

Arsenal v. Millwall

17 March 1945
Stamford Bridge, London

Football League South Cup semi-final
Attendance: 49,513

In this wartime cup competition Millwall qualified to meet Chelsea in the final of the League South Cup at Wembley on 7 April, but they almost threw away their chance by rashly conceding two penalty kicks in the last fifteen minutes of the semi-final.

Outplaying an all-powerful Arsenal side, the Lions grabbed their chance with both hands halfway through the first half to score the only goal of the game. Arsenal started the game with a determined attack on the Millwall goal and it appeared they were all set on a comfortable victory when Farquhar sent in a shot from close range that was held by guest player Sam Bartram (from Charlton).

It was some minutes before the Lions could get a grip on the encounter, in which the defence was severely tried in holding the Arsenal attack. Some relief for the beleaguered rearguard came when Ludford received the ball from well outside the box and struck a long range shot that narrowly missed.

From then on Millwall's defence were holding the Gunners' attack, and were forcing the ball upfield. It was through one of these sorties that the all important goal materialised. Scot Tommy Brown gained possession, eluded two Arsenal defenders and put through a perfect pass to his centre forward. Jimmy Jinks fastened on to the ball and his perfectly aimed shot flashed into the net to put the Lions one up after 20 minutes.

Millwall now went all out to increase this lead, and it was only a grand save by Marks that prevented them for doing so, as Rawlings crashed in a left foot drive. However, it was Arsenal who nearly drew level when Drake, receiving the ball from Wrigglesworth's pass sent in a powerful shot from point-blank range that struck Bartram, the ball going behind for a corner.

From the resultant kick, the ball was nicely placed into the goalmouth where Stan Mortensen connected with a header, with the ball just grazing the bar on its way over. Arsenal missed another chance of equalising when Edelston had passed to Wrigglesworth, who being in front of an open goal shot yards wide – much to the disbelief of everyone.

In the second half Arsenal rearranged their forward line, Wrigglesworth appearing at outside right and Bastin wide on the left, but there was no real improvement in their attack, as play swung from end to end. It seemed that Tommy Brown would be certain to score as he raced up at terrific speed to put in a great shot that was going all the way before striking a defender.

The Lions were at this stage putting on the pressure and were very unfortunate to have a goal by another guest, Bert Brown, disallowed. The excitement became intense during the last fifteen minutes, during which Arsenal were awarded two penalties, and failed to score from either of them.

The first came when George Fisher brought down Wrigglesworth well inside the area, only for Mortensen to see Bartram pull off a great save from his fierce spot kick. Three minutes from the end, the Gunners had second chance to level when Ted Smith intercepted a pass with his hands. This time Hall was given the opportunity to score, but at this critical point he ballooned the ball over the top. Millwall ran out worthy winners and a large contribution to their success came from the two Browns – Albert, another guest from Charlton, and Tom, the former Hearts player – and brilliant work by Sam Bartram in goal.

Arsenal 0	Millwall 1	Referee: G. Clark (London)
	Jinks	

1945 Millwall Cup final team. From left to right, back row: Bill Moor, G. Phillips, Reg Dudley, George Fisher, Ted Smith, Sam Bartram, Tommy Brown, Bill Voisey, A.S. Williams, Joe Shaw, Jack Cock (manager). Front row: Sid Rawlings, Albert Brown, George Ludford, Jimmy Jinks, Len Tyler, George Carney (trainer).

1944/45:
FLSC (Group 2)

1	3 Feb	(a) Fulham W 3-1	Jinks (3)	8,000
2	10 Feb	(h) Brentford W 3-2	Phillips (2) Ludford	8,553
3	17 Feb	(a) Brighton&HA L 2-6	Williams, Hurrell	10,000
4	24 Feb	(h) Fulham W 1-0	Rippley	9,000
5	3 Mar	(a) Brentford D 2-2	Jinks (2)	11,830
6	10 Mar	(h) Brighton&HA W 1-0	Stevenson	12,200
SF	17 Mar	(Stamford Bridge) Arsenal W 1-0	Jinks	49,513
F	7 Apr	(Wembley) Chelsea L 0-2		90,000

Arsenal: Marks, Moody, Scott, Bastin, Hall, Hamilton, Farquhar, Edelston, Drake, Mortensen, Wrigglesworth.
Millwall: Bartram, Dudley, G. Fisher, Ludford, E. Smith, Tyler, Rawlings, A. Brown, Jinks, T. Brown, Medley.

NEWCASTLE UNITED v. MILLWALL

28 December 1946
St James Park, Newcastle.

Football League Second Division
Attendance: 53,000

For the second Christmas since the war, the Lions faced a gruelling time by having to play three games in four days with a home game versus Chesterfield on Christmas Day followed by the return fixture on Boxing Day, then a further slog north on the 28 December to meet the mighty Newcastle United. Both of Millwall's opponents were holding down positions in the top six, with the Lions struggling third from bottom.

Above most people's expectations Millwall grabbed three points from Chesterfield with a 1-1 draw at The Den followed by a splendid 3-2 victory at Saltergate, with Johnny Johnson getting two goals. This put the Lions in fine fettle for the game on Tyneside, where Millwall had a score to settle with the Geordies, for they had inflicted a crushing 4-1 defeat at Cold Blow Lane on opening day of the season in front of 39,287 spectators. The task facing Millwall looked very daunting, especially with Newcastle fielding such legends and future England internationals as Jackie Milburn, Len Shackleton, and Roy Bentley. The rest of their team were strewn with top calibre players and it appeared that there was not a weak link in the side. Millwall did not need telling that a tough game lay ahead, although manager Jack Cock, who had been involved in big games himself as a player, was unmoved by this clash, being brave enough to say to Newcastle director and manager Stan Seymour, 'My boys are playing so well now that we shall beat you today'.

They say that fortune favours the brave and Jack's prophecy came true. Just to show that their Boxing Day win at Chesterfield was no fluke, Millwall beat Newcastle before 53,000 spectators by two clear goals. The Lions put up a storming game in the first half and literally ran the home side off their feet to the general surprise of the large crowd, with the magnificent Benny Fenton in outstanding form. An 11th-minute lead was established when Wilfred Heathcote took advantage of a mistake by Smith, who miskicked a long through ball, to score with ease and silence a raucous Geordie crowd. Against all the odds Millwall increased their lead just before the interval when Newcastle goalkeeper Swinburne was penalised for taking too many steps. After a protracted delay the kick was taken and Smith made his second telling contribution to the Lions cause by handling the ball in an attempt to prevent a goal. Instead of allowing the effort to stand the referee awarded a penalty kick. It was left to Tommy Brown to thump it home a minute before the half-time whistle.

Newcastle came out for the second half really fired up. Millwall having some idea of what to expect decided upon a 'what we have we hold' policy. Defending as if their lives depended upon it, they repelled United time and time again, although as Newcastle became desperate to salvage something from the game, the Lions still found time to launch some strong attacks of their own.

As the home team began to turn the screws, the Newcastle fans cranked up the noise level. Their team responded well and fought hard to wipe out the arrears. With time running out, however, the Millwall defenders were in commanding form and, after a capital display by Purdie in the Millwall goal (despite the fact that he was knocked out for his troubles), managed to keep the home side from getting even a consolation. This match, the first in which the Magpies had failed to score that season, galvanised Millwall somewhat as they struggled for the rest of the campaign before climbing to the relatively safe position of eighteenth.

Newcastle United 0

Millwall 2
Heathcote
Brown (pen)

Referee: H. Berry (Huddersfield)

Millwall gained ample revenge over Newcastle United when picking up their second away win in two days over Christmas 1946. The excellent 2-0 victory came in front of a crowd of 53,000. One of the scorers, Tommy Brown, is pictured in the front row (fifth from the left) in this team group.

1946/47:

P	W	D	L	F	A	PTS
42	14	8	20	56	79	36

Second Division
Eighteenth Place
Manager: Jack Cock
Top goalscorer: Johnnie Johnson (10)
Highest Attendance: WBA 46,000

Newcastle United: Swinburn, Burke, Graham, Woodburn, Smith, Wright, Milburn, Bentley, Wayman, Pearson.
Millwall: Purdie, Tyler, Williams, Fenton, Brolly, Kelly, Johnson Jinks, Heathcote, Brown, Mansfield.

MILLWALL v. NOTTS COUNTY

22 October 1948
The Den

Football League Second Division
Attendance: 45,642

(Adapted from a contemporary report.)

Millwall's record post-war crowd witnessed a remarkable result against a team that had scored nine goals in their two previous games, with England international Tommy Lawton the star. The record receipts from the large crowd were £3,177 15s 9d. Those monies went towards the building of the new main stand, the work starting after this match. With a well-merited 3-2 victory over the glamour boys of Notts County, the Lions in their Den proved that all things are possible in those days of 'Alice in Wonderland' football and attempts to buy success the easy way with hard cash.

What great stuff this match was, with glimpses of football of the best vintage. It pitted sound defences against scheming forwards, all looking for that vital opening to seize a chance. Much was expected of the County's scoring machine, but it was not their day. Indeed, they were never allowed to settle down and it came as no surprise, after Sewell had scored in the first few minutes, that Millwall took command and dictated the play.

Two wonderful headers by centre forward Jimmy Constantine, who had complete mastery throughout of harassed Alan Brown, started a period of brilliant Millwall football, and suddenly Notts were looking yards slower than their opponents. However, a brisk effort, calling to mind the sharp snort of a goods engine, brought Tommy Lawton into action with a beautiful flick for Johnston to head an equalising goal, but their success was short lived, and with the second half just three minutes old, George Fisher settled the day with a glorious effort.

The Notts hopes flickered on occasions, but they were doused with an almost audible sizzle by the hard clean tackling of the Millwall defence, in which Evans and McMilllen were brilliant. The story of the game is simply that the Millwall team were altogether too smart on the ball for a County defence that was very slow in moving and tackling. It was Millwall's day and their performance was a grand one. The Lions were a pleasure to watch in those trying times.

1948/49:

P	W	D	L	F	A	PTS
42	17	11	14	63	64	45

Second Division
Eighth Place
Manager: Charlie Hewitt
Top Goalscorer: Jimmy Constantine (23)
Highest Attendance: Notts County 45,642
Average Attendance: 24,629

Millwall 3
Constantine (2)
G. Fisher

Notts County 2
Sewell
Johnston

Referee: S.E. Law

Notts County centre forward Tommy Lawton and Millwall's centre half McMillan battle it out. McMillan won both battles when Millwall 'done the double' over Notts County at the Den and Meadow Lane. This tussle was watched by Millwall's biggest League crowd of 45,642.

Finlayson (Millwall goalkeeper) saves from Tommy Lawton (Notts County). Evans for Millwall covers up.

Millwall: Finlayson, Evans, Tyler, Reeves, McMillen, Brolly, Johnson, Hurrell, Constantine, Jones, G. Fisher.
Notts County: Brown, Southwell, Howe, Gannon, Brown, Adamson, Houghton, Sewell, Lawton, Hold, Johnston.

Millwall v. Glasgow Celtic

25 April 1949
The Den

W. Moor's Benefit
Attendance: 19,875

Bill Moor kept up the family tradition of being groundsman to Millwall FC. Succeeding his father Elijah, who was first employed in 1886, Bill then followed in his footsteps in 1919 up until the late 1950s and was given a well-earned benefit match against Celtic, a fine side who, as one half of the 'Old Firm', had built a great tradition within the Scottish game.

This meeting was a great attraction for the South London club – and Bill Moor in particular. Celtic were managed by the legendary centre forward of yesteryear James McGrory, and at the time they had won the Scottish League championship nineteen times and were Scottish cup winners on fifteen occasions. Their team contained five internationals: Miller, Mallan, Macaulay, Johnson (all of Scotland) and from Northern Ireland came the influential Charlie Tully. With the appetite thus whetted, a decent crowd of just under 20,000 looked forward to an entertaining game.

Although the spectators were treated to five goals, they unfortunately witnessed a tough and often bruising game of football that was played in very sunny but windy conditions. A below-strength Millwall team surprised the large crowd by pulling out the best in their play and at one stage during the first half they led 3-0.

The first goal came after 10 minutes when Taffy Evans opened the scoring. Maguire, the Celtic left-back, became the first casualty when he was carried off injured with a badly gashed leg that needed stitches, and was replaced by Tommy Doherty. The second goal was a cracker from another of the Lions' Welsh contingent Les Jones, whose shot entered the top corner of the net. Soon afterwards, Willie Hurrell netted Millwall's third when cashing in on a mistake by his countryman Miller, the Celts' 'keeper.

The state of affairs at half-time no doubt encouraged Celtic to try a bit harder, and were duly rewarded with two quick-fire responses, both of which came from the penalty spot, and were scored by Johnny Paton, who was remembered by much of the crowd as a guest player for Millwall during the war. The first spot-kick came when Frank Reeves – more in enthusiasm than malice – was adjudged to have fouled his opponent, and the second award was given for reasons that no one but the referee could fathom.

In truth the second half was a shocker, resembling more of a game of rugby than a match under association rules. The official appeared to lose control and with numerous infringements and stoppages any free flowing football was out of the question, which upset and disappointed the fans. The decision that caused much of the resentment was the award of the second penalty. From there on the many incidents that occurred were very regrettable, the result of one was a very bad injury to young goalkeeper Malcolm Finlayson, who collapsed in the bath after the game and was taken to The Miller Hospital as a precautionary measure.

The one good thing to come out this unsavoury event was that the gross receipts for the game were £1,539 0s 3d. However, Celtic took £691 and the taxman £500, while Bill was left with only £350.

Millwall 3
Evans
Jones
Hurrell

Glasgow Celtic 2
Patton (2 pens)

Referee: Mr V. Rae (London)

Above left: Millwall groundsman Bill Moor.
Above right: John Evans scored the first goal against Glasgow Celtic. He played for Millwall between 1946 and 1950 making 77 appearances and scoring 2 goals.

Left: Willie Hurrell put Millwall 3-0 up. He joined Millwall in 1944/45 and went on to make 126 appearances between 1946 and 1953 scoring 33 goals.

1948/49:

P	W	D	L	F	A	PTS
42	17	11	14	63	64	45

Third Division (South)
Eighth Place
Manager: Charles Hewitt
Top Goalscorer: Jimmy Constantine (23)
Highest Attendance: Notts County 45,642

Millwall: Finlayson, G. Fisher, Tyler, Brolly, Reeves, Bradley, Evans, Hurrell, Constantine, L. Jones, Mansfield.
Glasgow Celtic: Miller, Maguire (T. Doherty), Baillie, Mallan, Bowden, Macaulay, Johnston, J. Doherty, Weir, Tully, Paton.

QUEENS PARK RANGERS v. MILLWALL

6 January 1951
Loftus Road

FA Cup third round
Attendance: 25,777

If it was goals you wanted to see, then Millwall was the team to watch. In their last two games they beat Ipswich 4-0 and Gillingham 4-3. In this seven goal thriller against Second Division Rangers in the FA cup, Millwall came out on top. The Lions attacked straight from the whistle and Neary was nearly on the mark with a shot which just skimmed the outside of the post. For the first five minutes it was all Millwall as they tried to take advantage of Heath's nervousness at left back. In Rangers' first attack, Addinall had a chance but tried to dribble through instead of shooting first time and Finlayson was able to clear. Saphin punched a shot from Jones over the bar and from the corner Constantine headed only inches too high. Rangers nearly scored when Duggan broke through but Finlayson made a great save. Rangers made several raids but finished badly, Millwall got the ball into the net after Jones shot through from a pass by Neary but the winger was given off-side. Millwall took the lead when Jones drew the Rangers defence for Neary to exploit space on the left to shoot into the corner of the net after 26 minutes' play. Rangers drew level when Addinall secured the ball as it came down the middle and dribbled past two defenders before shooting home after 32 minutes. Millwall held the whip hand for most of the first half, and they continued to do so after the interval. After 8 minutes play, Constantine passed back to Neary, who sent in a pile driver that gave Saphin no chance. Later Neary missed a clear cut chance, shooting past the post when unmarked. The game was showing signs of becoming rough, with the trainers of both sides being kept busy. On the hour mark Millwall scored twice – first Johnson scored with a drive from the edge of the penalty area and then, before Rangers had recovered, Constantine shot past Saphin from right in front of the goal. Finlayson saved at point blank range from Addinall before Parkinson then scored for Rangers in the 64th minute, shooting over a crowd of players into the net. Parkinson scored for QPR from Waugh's centre eight minutes from time and with only three minutes remaining of play, Shepherd missed an easy chance to level the scores with Finlayson on the ground. Millwall went on to play First Division Fulham in the next round, losing 1-0 in front of 42,000.

1950/51: FA Cup

1	Nov 29	(a) Crystal Palace W 4-1	Johnson, Morgan, Neary, Constantine	14,817
2	Dec 9	(h) Bradford D 1-1	Neary	22,844
R	Dec 13	(a) Bradford W 1-0	Morgan	11,507
3	Jan 6	(a) QPR W 4-3	Neary 2, Johnson, Constantine	25,777
4	Jan 27	(h) Fulham L 0-1		42,170

Third Division (South)
Fifth Place
Manager: Charles Hewitt
Top Goalscorer: Jimmy Constantine (26)
Highest Attendance: Norwich 35,000
Average Attendance: 20,164

Queens Park Rangers 3
Addinall
Parkinson (2)

Millwall 4
Neary (2)
Johnson
Constantine

Referee: E.S. Vickery (Bristol)

Parkinson, Queens Park Rangers' inside right, on his hands and knees and Finlayson, the Millwall goalkeeper, prostate, after a collision in the Millwall goalmouth.

Left: Johnny Johnson scored from the edge of the area. *Right:* Frank (Brown Bomber) Neary scored 2 goals. His pile driver was a little too much for the 'keeper. Signed from Orient by Charlie Hewitt for £6,000 between 1950 and 1954 he scored 59 goals in 142 appearances.

Queens Park Rangers: Saphin, Poppitt, Heath, Nicholas, Woodward, Parkinson, Waugh, Duggan, Addinall, Hatton, Shepherd.

Millwall: Finlayson, Jardine, G. Fisher, Short, Bowler, Reeves, Johnson, Constantine, Neary, Morgan, L. Jones.

Ipswich Town v. Millwall

21 March 1953   Football League Third Division (South)
Portman Road, Ipswich   Attendance: 13,793

The saying 'what goes around comes around' could well have applied to this game, and in particular to the Ipswich Town manager at the time, Scott Duncan. This was the same Scott Duncan who was in charge at Manchester United when his team sent Millwall down on that fateful day back in 1934. With the nineteenth anniversary of that game on the horizon the Lions, who were going well in their particular division, exacted a delayed revenge on Duncan and his new charges. Coming off a disappointing home result against Leyton Orient the previous week, Millwall were to hit back at their critics in the best possible manner.

Falling behind to a goal from Town's evergreen wing-half Tom Parker after 12 minutes, it appeared that Millwall were again to fail the test. However, this early reverse had the desired effect as they displayed a fine quality of football that had elevated them into the promotion race; and before half-time was reached the Lions had raced into a 3-1 lead with two goals from Johnny Hartburn, whose brace was separated by centre forward Allan Monkhouse's effort.

Unfortunately for Ipswich they lost left-back Dave Deacon prior to the interval with a damaged ankle, and from that moment the home side were always going to be under severe pressure. As one would expect, Millwall took advantage of their extra man.

Jack Parry, Ipswich's Welsh goalkeeper who had conceded three goals in his one appearance for his country, would be picking the ball out the net on three more occasions during the second half as the visitors dominated all areas of the pitch. They were aided and abetted in this by some terrible Ipswich defending as Monkhouse took his second goal and Freddy Smith scored two.

This defeat was Town's heaviest of the season, and Millwall's best result since they hammered Aldershot 7-1 in the FA Cup earlier in the campaign. This was the third occasion that the Lions had won 6-1 on opposing grounds in the Football League: the others came at Crystal Palace in 1926/27 and at Manchester City in 1938/39.

1952/53:

P	W	D	L	F	A	PTS
46	24	14	8	82	44	62

Third Division (South)
Second Place
Manager: Charlie Hewitt
Top Goalscorer: Johnny Shepherd (15)
Average Attendance: 19,109

Ipswich Town 1   **Millwall 6**   **Referee:** Mr J.R. Dunbar (Stapleford)
Parker   *Hartburn (2)*
                             Monkhouse (2)
                             Smith (2)

Above left: John Hartburn scorer of two goals in the first half. He was signed from Watford he played 112 games and scored 30 goals between 1950 and 1954.
Above right: Alan Monkhouse scored the second and fourth goals. He played 71 games and scored 25 goals between 1949 and 1954. *Right:* Fred Smith who scored two goals in the 6-1 win. The scotsman who signed from Sheffield United played 100 games for Millwall and scored 22 goals between 1952 and 1956.

Ipswich Town: Parry, Acres, Deacon, Myles, Clarke, Parker, Gaynor, Brown, Higgins, Elsworthy, Ball.
Millwall: Finlayson, Jardine, Fisher, Reeves, Bowler, Short, Neary, Smith, Monkhouse, Saward, Hartburn.

MILLWALL v. MANCHESTER UNITED

5 October 1953　　　　　　　　　　　Opening of the Floodlights
The Den, London　　　　　　　　　　Attendance: 20,082

The opening of The Den's new £15,000 floodlights brought the famous 'Busby Babes' of Manchester United to the South London ground and a spectacular win for the Lions fans to witness. The President of the Football League, Mr Arthur Drewry, had the honour of switching on the lights for the 20,000 crowd.

United, the League Champions in 1952, were top draw opponents for Third Division Millwall for this historic occasion. Millwall were not overawed, however, as this was the two sides' third meeting in ten months – the Lions had held the Reds to a 4-4 draw at The Den in a friendly the previous May and narrowly lost 1-0 in an FA Cup tie in January.

The supporters were to see the first night game under lights, and the new era dawning for the future of football. The match got under way at 7.40 pm and the slick-moving Manchester team were soon put off their stride by the more rugged play of Millwall. Passes started going astray and the game developed into more of a scramble. After only 9 minutes, Alex Jardine gave Millwall the lead from the penalty spot. The goal that put Millwall further ahead came about when Wood only just managed to tip over a Smith header from a John Short's cross. From the resultant corner, a high in-swinging cross delivered by Alan Monkhouse deceived Wood (who appeared to be obstructed as he attempted to catch it) and the ball dropped into the goal.

Between these Millwall goals Taylor, who had been one of United's most dangerous forwards, had headed the equaliser. United cast all caution to wind and threw everything into all-out attack towards the end but Tony Brewer, the Millwall 'keeper, was not to be beaten again. Left-half Jackie Blanchflower was the United star on the night, while Brewer and Bowler both shone for Millwall. The return of Frank Neary to lead the Millwall attack was not a success, his unnecessarily robust play brought him nothing more than a cut head late in the game during which both Jardine and Johnson went off with leg injuries, with Hartburn and Quinn deputising.

1953/54:

P	W	D	L	F	A	PTS
46	19	9	18	74	77	47

Third Division (South)
Twelfth Place
Manager; Charles Hewitt
Top Goalscorer: George Stobbart (17)
Highest Attendance: Crystal Palace 21,952

Millwall 2　　　　　　　　**Manchester United 1**　　　　**Referee:** R.J. Leafe (Nottingham)
Jardine (pen)　　　　　　　　*Taylor*
Monkhouse

The floodlight posts and scoreboard provide extra 'grandstands' for the spectators packed into the Den, New Cross, London, watching Millwall play Newcastle United in the FA Cup fourth round.

Manchester United paid three visits to The Den in 1953. The first occasion was in January for a Cup tie which United won 1-0. The following May the two sides played out a 4-4 friendly game and in October they met for the grand opening of the new floodlights. The photograph on the left shows some action from the FA Cup encounter.

Millwall: Brewer, Jardine (Hartburn), G Fisher, Short, Bowler, Heydon, Johnson (Quinn), Smith, Neary, Stobbart, Monkhouse.
Manchester United: Wood, Foulkes, Byrne, Whitefoot, Chilton, Blanchflower, McFarlane, Aston, Taylor, Rowley, McShane.

CRYSTAL PALACE v. MILLWALL

31 March 1961
Selhurst Park

Football League Division Four
Attendance: 37,774

Over the Easter weekend 53,000 spectators watched the eagerly awaited south-east derby with over 37,000 at Selhurst Park, still a Division Four crowd record. Crystal Palace were sitting at the top of the division, and Millwall had a chance of closing the ten point gap. Millwall won 2-0 at Selhurst but the score reversed at the Den. This meant that Millwall had to spend another season in the Fourth Division. But on Good Friday it was Millwall's day. No nonsense Millwall dominated the play from the first minute with their bang-it-down-the-field policy and Palace were made to look just another ordinary side. It was the solid defence which controlled the game. Best forward on the field was undoubtedly little Joey Broadfoot who whipped through the Palace defence whenever he got the ball and dominated proceedings. After 14 minutes, Millwall took the lead when Dave Jones gathered one of the long clearances. He passed it on to Alf Ackerman who rounded Choules before flicking it back to Jones who struck it first time into the corner of the net. Reg Davies, in the Millwall goal, did well to save from Gavin and Summersby before Millwall scored again. Another long clearance bounced between Choules and Ackerman into an open space and Peter Burridge ran through to score with an angled shot from the left-hand side of the penalty box. The only downfall to the Lions' victory was the injury to left-back Pat Brady who came out of a tackle with Gavin with a thigh injury and was forced to miss the rest of the Easter games. Burridge's goal tally of 35 League goals at the end of the season was a record that still stands although Teddy Sheringham came close with 33 in 1990.

Davies leaps up at another cross to stop the Palace attack. Davies went up high to push a centre over the head of George Petchey and Ray Brady.

Crystal Palace 0	Millwall 2	Referee: E.T. Jennings (Worcester)
	Jones	
	Burridge	

Joey Broadfoot (left) and Dave Jones (right) working out during training.

Dave Bumpstead stops the ball crossing the line after George Petchey beats Reg Davies.

Crystal Palace: Davies, Jackson, P Brady, Bumpstead, R Brady, Anderson, Broadfoot, Jones, Ackerman, Burridge, Spears.

Millwall: Rouse, McNichol, Noakes, Long, Choules, Petchey, Gavin, Summersby, Uphill, Byrne, Heckman

MILLWALL v. PETERBOROUGH

22 April 1961
The Den

Division Four
Attendance: 18,503

Millwall fans could see a re-run of the game that night as it was televised for *Match of the Day*. Peterborough, already assured of promotion, were racing away with the division, six points ahead, with a game in hand of their nearest rivals Crystal Palace. Peterborough were the league's highest goalscorers with 120 goals and with Millwall lying sixth with 91 goals, this was all set for an attacking game. Peter Burridge was the leading goalscorer with a record 33 goals and was looking forward to adding to his tally. Peterborough having their fourth game in eight days, were always the more skilful side building up their attacks. But Millwall, with most of their team playing for a new contract for next season, performed with rare spirit. In the last twenty minutes Millwall had to defend almost continuously while Posh earned 16 corners. On one occasion McNamee ran through and pushed a gentle shot wide of goalkeeper Reg Davies, but Dave Bumpstead had time to get back and kick off the line, followed by a shot from Emery rebounded from the underside of the bar. The strong man of the Millwall side was centre half Ray Brady and, although beaten for height by Terry Bly, he won a good share of the high balls down the middle. Bumpstead was always in the thick of things. Peterborough were never ahead; six minutes from the start an Ackerman-Spears move allowed Jones to score for Millwall. After twenty minutes Bly pushed a centre from McNamee past a postrate Davies, but Millwall went ahead again in the 33rd minute. The ball travelled from Bumpstead to Ackerman and on to Burridge for an easy goal. Soon after, Denis Jackson made an appalling mistake when his miskick let McNamee in. Just before half-time goalkeeper Walls missed a high centre from Broadfoot and Spears made it 3-2. After the interval Burridge headed home a Jackson free kick, and fifteen minutes from time Bly got a second goal for Peterborough. Youths invaded the pitch every time Millwall scored in the first half, so referee Mann issued a warning that if it happened again he would abandon the game. The children kept out of trouble in the second half. Peterborough went on to win the Championship, and Peter Burridge gained a new goalscoring record for Millwall.

1960/61:

P	W	D	L	F	A	PTS
46	21	8	17	97	86	50

Division: Four
Sixth Place
Manager: R. Gray
Top Goalscorer: Peter Burridge
Highest Attendance: Peterborough 18,503
Average Attendance: 9,703

Millwall 4
Jones
Burridge (2)
Spears

Peterborough 3
Bly (2)
McNamee

Referee: R.H. Mann (Worcester)

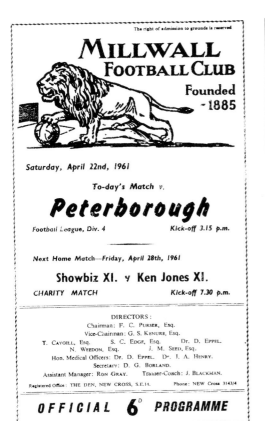

Above right: Peter Burridge scored the winner and made a new goal scoring record. He was signed by Millwall from Leyton Orient and between 1960 and 1962 he scored 64 goals in 93 games.

Below: The referee warns the kids about running on the pitch.

Millwall: Davies, Jackson, P. Brady, Bumpstead, R. Brady, Vaesson, Broadfoot, Jones, Ackerman, Burridge, Spears.
Peterborough: Walls, Whittaker, Walker, Rayner, Rigby, Ripley, Hails, Emery, Bly, Smith, McNamee.

BARROW v. MILLWALL

30 April 1962
Holker Street Ground, Barrow-in-Furness

Football League Fourth Division
Attendance: 5,080

This was the third consecutive away game Millwall had to play in their quest for Third Division football. The first at Darlington, where the Lions won 5-1 – Garry Townend obtaining a hat-trick and Pat Terry scoring for the sixth successive match. Easter saw a visit to Exeter with Townend again scoring in a 1-1 draw that secured promotion.

Now they faced the long trip to Barrow, where a point would guarantee them the Fourth Division Championship. The result was duly achieved, but in a most contentious way. A hotly disputed goal by Peter Burridge gave them the point they needed, but Barrow made Millwall fight every inch of way to earn the right to lift the trophy. With the Lions trailing 2-1 with 16 minutes to go, they grabbed the all-important equaliser when Burridge was allowed to run through a static Barrow defence that stood like statues waiting for the non-existent whistle to sound. The forward duly slotted home Millwall's second. Referee Edge allowed the goal to stand and waved away Barrow's strong protests – a decision that surprised even some of the Millwall players.

The Millwall team in celebratory mood.

Barrow 2
Brown
Armstrong

Millwall 2
Terry
Burridge

Referee: A. Edge (Liverpool)

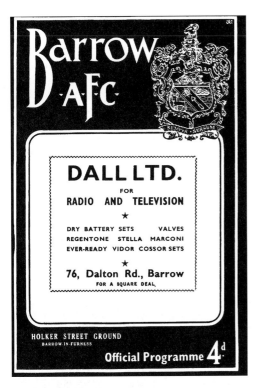

Peter Burridge holds aloft the Fourth Division Championship trophy.

The game had started ever so well for the home side when Gordon Brown had opened the scoring to give Barrow the lead in the 37th minute. It was centre forward Pat Terry who equalised with his thirteenth goal in seventeen appearances for the Lions with a first time drive, but it looked to be all over when Jimmy Armstrong again hammered Barrow in front with the northern side's second. It seemed that Millwall would have to settle for promotion, but then came Burridge's unusual goal and Millwall clinched their first title in twenty-four years.

Millwall had got their reward, but the way it was obtained left a bitter taste in many a Barrow mouth. The home support all felt that Burridge's goal should have been disallowed and roundly booed Mr Edge and his linesmen at the end of the match.

1961/62:

P	W	D	L	F	A	PTS
44	23	10	11	87	62	56

Fourth Division
Champions
Manager: Ron Gray
Top Goalscorer: Peter Burridge (23)
Highest Attendance: Exeter 19,666

Barrow: Caine, Arrowsmith, Cahill, Hale, Robinson, Clark, Maddison, Darwin, Dixon, Brown, Kemp.
Millwall: Davies, Gilchrist, P. Brady, Obeney, R. Brady, A. Anderson, Broadfoot, Townend, Terry, Jones, Burridge.

Millwall v. Fulham

11 January 1965
The Den, London

FA Cup third round
Attendance: 31,339

Fourth Division Millwall were this season's giant-killers in the FA Cup after beating First Division Fulham in a third round replay at The Den amid scenes of happy pandemonium, in which Dave Harper – Millwall's right half who had been told his injury-plagued career was over the season before – was the unlikely hero.

It was 'Harper, Harper' for whom an estimated 35,000 fans – many had burst into The Den through a broken gate – sang their salutes in the mad minutes of joy at the end. Their exultation was as much for Harper's courage as his goal, a goal that finally sent fighting, frantic Fulham out of the cup.

Harper was hurt before half-time, then knocked out in a collision in which he injured his hip, and on two occasions he tried to resume before being led sadly to the dressing room. It seemed that Millwall must fight on with only ten men, but as the teams came out for the second half a tremendous cheer rose above the continuous din as his lone, limping figure followed the team out with one hand clasped to his side.

Harper did nothing but wander wearily in attack for the next 22 minutes, but if Fulham had ignored his presence they were soon to regret it as he got his injury-ravaged frame to the ball after Barry Rowan had slid back a Dennis John cross out of reach of three Fulham defenders for Harper to lunge painfully forward and sidefoot the opening goal. Poor old Dave couldn't have realised what he had done as the hugs of congratulations must have hurt him – although a dazed Harper's delighted grin showed he would endure it again for another goal. But he and his colleague had to wait until two minutes from time, before this tie was finally settled.

Then, in an isolated break from Fulham's frantic siege on the Millwall goal, Kenny Jones managed to get away and cross the ball to Harper, who somehow survived a crunching tackle to juggle the ball a yard away to Rowan, who happily finished off the West London team once and for all. Invading fans threatened to mar the evening as they came on to the pitch with a small amount of time still to play and the Millwall players were anxiously shepherding off hundreds of supporters so that the last formal seconds could be cherished in a typical Millwall roar that would make every dockland rafters ring.

Fulham trailed despondently off a pitch on which they had been found so wanting. They knew they had only themselves to blame after being 3-1 up in the first match, but they had let the game slide and the initiative pass to opponents from much lower in the League. They could have had three up again in this replay before Millwall scored, but in too many places they lacked the fighting edge that turns cup-ties. That being said, Bobby Robson and George Cohen were magnificent, Jim Langley was a mud-spattered apparition of inspired aggression as he roared late into attack, while John Dempsey, an eighteen-year-old centre half had a plucky and polished debut in what was a baptism of fire.

These lone efforts were not enough to equal the burning zeal for victory that made every Millwall man – particularly Wilson, Curran and John – seem each ten foot tall and willing to put in lionhearted tackling when required. Captained by vociferous and bellicose Harry Cripps, a full-back who would be nobody's idea of a classy footballer, Millwall did not try to out think the tremendous weight of experience and knowledge that Fulham boasted. They simply ignored it.

It was a classic cup-tie of break neck football, with head down running, heedless tackling and an atmosphere of raucous hostility. The scene was set before the match

---

Millwall 2
Harper
Rowan

Fulham 0

Referee: Mr N.C. Burtenshaw (Norfolk)

Fulham's Rodney Marsh (left) and centre forward Reg Stratton on the attack near the Millwall goalmouth during their FA Cup third round replay match in London.

when thousands besieged the ground, and in their urgency in gaining entrance they broke through a 12ft gate and hundreds poured and roared through the gap before mounted police could seal it.

The police ordered the turnstiles closed five minutes after the kick off, with the crowd now packed onto terraces and crouched around the touchlines. When the game got underway the Millwall fans must have wondered whether their efforts were worth it as England captain Johnny Haynes sent in a fine shot that was only inches wide. It was Haynes again who created a chance when he spun to hit the ball at Stepney's chest, and then Fulham again nearly took the lead that their early dominance deserved when Reg Stratton hit the inside of the post only for the ball to rebound out.

However, the second half belonged to Millwall and to the legend of competition in which all men are equal – but the likes of brave Millwall are a bit more equal than others. Billy Gray the Millwall manager said afterwards that Harper was taken to hospital for some precautionary x-rays, and added, 'The lads did what I wanted in the second half. It was not going well at first and I had to give them a pep talk. Afterwards they gave 100 per cent and ran themselves into the ground.'

'It was donkeys against thoroughbreds.'
    Bobby Robson, Fulham and England
'Yes, the donkeys had two chances, and still lost.'
    Billy Gray, Millwall manager

Millwall: Stepney, Gilchrist, Cripps, Harper, Wilson, Gough, Rowan, Whitehouse, D. Jones, Curran, John.
Fulham: Macedo, Cohen, Langley, Robson, Dempsey, Brown, Key, Marsh, Stratton, Haynes, Chamberlain.

Notts County v. Millwall

29 April 1965
County Ground, Meadow Lane

Football League Fourth Division
Attendance: 7,322

Billy Gray led Millwall back to the Third Division a year after their relegation. The team not only won promotion, but finished runners-up to Brighton. Gray, who won a cup medal with Nottingham Forest in 1959, returned to Trentside to end his playing career in a blaze of glory. Len Julians, another former Forest man, scored the first goal.

Hundreds of Millwall fans stormed across the pitch to cheer and chair the thirty-eight-year-old player-manager and refused to disperse until the team took a grandstand bow. Millwall needed one point from this, their last match, to pip Tranmere – with whom they were level on points but behind on goal difference – and go up with Brighton, York and Oxford. Gray said 'It is a proud night for myself and the boys. They have all worked hard to achieve promotion.' Instead of packing their defence Millwall gambled with progressive football that Gray had demanded all season, and won deservedly.

In the first half, County showed surprising urgency. Pace hit a stanchion with one searing attempt, and in a 13th minute a mixture of luck and judgement allowed the Millwall defence to block two shots before Rayner's header dropped safely into Stepney's arms. Suddenly, Millwall found their rhythm and not many defences could have done much to prevent the opening goal. It came from a splendid move as a Rowan cross from the right saw Julians burst into the area, coolly shake off the attentions of Gibson and Coates, kill the ball instantly and shoot past Smith in the 31st minute.

It was fitting that Gray should have the vital role in the decisive goal, which came after 50 minutes. Playing on the left wing, the man who came out of retirement eight matches before, sent over a pinpoint centre from which Rowan scored with a flying header. However, some of the risks Millwall took could have proved disastrous, as County pressed forward in the second half. Edwards scooped an easy chance over the bar from five yards, but he made amends in the 83rd minute after receiving a short pass from Pace to score. With the Lions still reeling from conceding the goal, Sheridan nearly equalised shortly afterwards when he thumped his shot against a Millwall post.

By the end Millwall were back in command, contemptuously testing Smith with some rasping shots. Yet, only a month before, Millwall had been eight points behind Tranmere, who led the Fourth Division. Their

Barry Rowan. His flying header gave the Lions the two points for promotion.

Notts County 1	Millwall 2	Referee: E. Norman (Blackburn)
Edwards	*Julians*	
	Rowan	

Celebrating promotion at County.

fighting climb with 16 points from the last 10 games pulled them through – the team's last defeat of the campaign being 16 games before at Tranmere on 19 February. The Notts County result was doubly rewarding: on 25 March, manager Gray had protested after the game at Meadow Lane had been abandoned at half-time with Millwall leading 2-1.

1964/65:

P	W	D	L	F	A	PTS
46	23	16	7	78	45	62

Fourth Division
Second Place
Player-manager: Billy Gray
Top Goalscorer: Hugh Curran (18)
Highest Attendance: Rochdale 15,359
Average Attendance: 9,272

Notts County: Smith, Hampton, Bircumshaw, Sheridan, Gibson, Coates, Flower, Edwards, Pace, Rayner, Bates.
Millwall: Stepney, John, Cripps; Jones, Snowdon, Wilson, Rowan, Gilchrist, Julians, Curran, Gray.

MILLWALL v. HULL CITY

28 December 1965
The Den

Football League Third Division
Attendance: 17,184

High-spending Hull's twenty-four hour taste of life at the top turned sour on them as magnificent Millwall reclaimed the leadership of the Third Division. This tense, tough ice-age spectacle had Hull skipper Andy Davidson claiming even before it got underway: 'It is ridiculous to let the game go on. Conditions are really dangerous.' When it was all over, the ten who tumbled to defeat with him must have wished it hadn't.

Thirty-four teams before Hull had failed to clear this hurdle – the Lions in League combat in front of their own cheering, chanting Dockland fans. Millwall sped over the frost-bound Den like men with built-in skates. Hull, who fell behind as early as the 11th minute, never looked like breaking the sequence. The masterstroke that made Millwall a top team again was the inclusion of right winger Barry Rowan, restored to the side after being kept out of the Boxing Day promotion clash at Boothferry Park. Rowan's pinpoint centres led to all three goals. In his first burst he ran hard, checked, then hit over a centre that sent inside right Len Julians jetting in to head past Maurice Swan. After twenty-five minutes his run and centre ended with centre forward Hugh Curran hurtling through to head another goal. A Ken Houghton pile-driver that whistled past a post was the nearest £200,000 Hull got to breaking down a well-drilled Millwall defence, in which centre half Bryan Snowdon was outstanding.

With Hull's resistance broken they lost heart and all hope long before Rowan's 86th-minute cross gave left winger Billy Neil the opportunity to clamber above the Tigers' defence to head Millwall's third.

1965/66:

P	W	D	L	F	A	PTS
46	27	11	8	76	43	65

Third Division
Second Place
Manager: Billy Gray
Top Goalscorer: Len Julians (22)
Highest Attendance: Bournemouth 17,578

'Hull who had beaten us up there, didn't relish this meeting at all, and we really did make them look mediocre.'
Billy Neil, Millwall FC

Millwall 3
Julians
Curran
Neil

Hull City 0

Referee: D.W. Smith (Gloucester)

Left: Len Julians was a vastly experienced striker who was Millwall's leading goalscorer in two of his three full seasons at the club.

Below: Len Julians scores Millwall's first goal at the Den.

Millwall: Stepney, Gilchrist, Cripps, Jones, Snowdon, Wilson, Rowan, Julians, Curran, Jacks, Neil.
Hull City: Swan, Davidson, Sharpe, Jarvis, Milner, Simpkin, Henderson, Wagstaff, Chilton, Houghton, I. Butler.

Scunthorpe v. Millwall

12 March 1966
Old Showground

Football League Division Three
Attendance: 5,624

Millwall were second in the table, just one point behind leaders Hull City. The Irons would prove a tough away game, and sitting fifth in the division needed the points to maintain a promotion push at the end of the season. In this game, however, Millwall showed they were no pushovers and fought until the final whistle.

From the kick-off it became obvious that the breezy conditions would make control of the light ball difficult. Controlling the game from midfield would also be a telling factor, and in this respect United had two keen players in Keith Burkinshaw and Bobby Smith, who both showed up well early on. However, in the 10th minute United were to find themselves behind. It was rather a fortunate goal as tricky Millwall winger Billy Neil put in a high centre which goalkeeeper Geoff Sidebottom managed to get a hand to, but was unable to hold. The ball dropped handily to Eamon Dunphy who had a simple job to side foot into an empty net. By half-time United were back in the hunt. Millwall's lead had lasted until the 32nd minute when a shot by Johnny Colquhoun was deflected by Bryan Snowdon into his own goal. Again fortune played its part because Alex Stepney in goal appeared to have the effort well covered. The second period of play was to produce some exciting attacking football from both teams, with Scunthorpe particularly effective on the flanks, using Sloan and Colquhoun to provide the centres. Only four minutes into the second half United took the lead following a corner. Alex Stepney managed to punch the ball clear only as far as Bobby Smith, who volleyed the ball straight into the net. Millwall replied seven minutes later with a shot by Billy Neil, which some United fans thought had not crossed the line. However, the referee was right on the spot and had no hesitation awarding the goal. At 2-2 the game appeared to be well balanced but goals by Colquhoun and Barton in the 69th and 71st minute looked to have sewn things up for the home club. The first came after heavy Scunthorpe pressure. Young full-back Derek Hemstead put Colquhoun clear and the winger hit a perfect shot past Alex Stepney. Two minutes later the crowd were again roaring as Frank Barton hammered in a cross from the right wing. With defeat looming, Millwall showed the class which was to win them promotion. In the 76th minute they pulled one back as Billy Neil scored his second goal from

Ken Jones scored in the last minute to equalise. He was signed from Southend United and between 1964 and 1970 appeared 193 and 4 sub times scoring 13 goals.

Scunthorpe United 4	Millwall 4	Referee: Mr J. Mitchell (Prescot)
Barton	*Dunphy*	
Colquhoun	*Neil (2)*	
Smith, Snowdon (o.g.)	*Jones*	

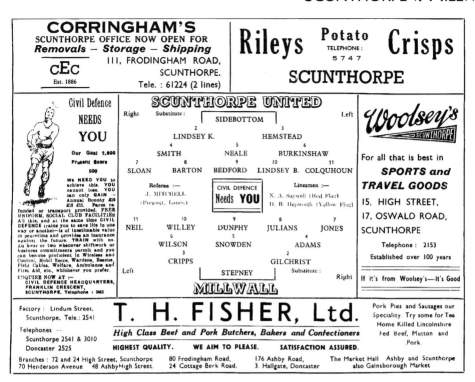

a breakaway. That was the signal for the visitors to press forward and it needed some stout defending to keep them at bay. It seemed the Irons would hold out, but in the last minute of the game they cracked, when a Ken Jones cross shot levelled matters. At four goals each Scunthorpe had again been caught by a late Millwall comeback, but nevertheless everyone had witnessed an excellent game.

1965/66

P	W	D	L	F	A	PTS
46	27	11	8	76	43	65

Division: Three
Second Place
Manager: W.P. Gray/B. Fenton
Top Goalscorer: Len Julians (22)
Highest Attendance: Bournemouth 17,578
Average Attendance: 13,919

Scunthorpe United: Sidebottom, K. Lindsay, Hemstead, Smith, Neale, Burkinshaw, Sloan, Barton, Bedford, B. Lindsay, Colquhoun.
Millwall: Stepney, Gilchrist, Cripps, Adams, Snowdon, Wilson, Jones, Julians, Dunphy, Willey, Neil.

WALSALL v. MILLWALL

7 May 1966
Fellows Park

Football League Division Three
Attendance: 11,224

It's promotion again for the second successive season. Millwall moved into the Second Division after outplaying Walsall. The players sang 'Glory, Glory' and new manager Benny Fenton, said 'They looked pretty good today.' It was a victory, too, for ex-manager Billy Gray, who had moved on to Brentford. It was he who had welded Millwall into a team in every sense, well-drilled in defence and cool and purposeful in attack. Hull City and Millwall, both now assured of promotion, were the only teams to have won at Walsall in the league that season. But there was never any doubt about Millwall's victory once they had weathered Walsall's early pressure and scored through Len Julians. Dunphy headed in a right wing cross and in the second half Millwall kept in command. Brown held off Bennett's challenge to lob a third and Julians flicked in a fourth while the home defence waited for an offside decision. Millwall's best work, however, was in defence where the tall Wilson and Snowdon cut out Walsall's hopeful high crosses. Stepney, watched by a Wolves scout and Northampton manager Dave Bowen, made goalkeeping look easy. The only time Stepney was beaten was from Middleton's penalty which came too late to help Walsall. Julians and Dunphy worked intelligently together in midfield for Millwall, with right-winger Barry Rowan showing speed and thrust. Gregg was just about the best for an out-of-touch Walsall until he limped off near the end. Benny Fenton beamed all the way home from Walsall, for his players had welcomed him with a red carpet 4-1 win that cancelled those mathematical doubts about Millwall's march to the Second Division. Fenton said, 'We played very well. I had no fears for our future in the Second Division.' Chairman Micky Purser reckoned, 'Promotion from the Fourth Division and this successful run in the third meant £10,000 to us in bigger gates and smaller travelling bills.' It should be even better next season. We have local clashes with Charlton and Crystal Palace and matches with teams like Blackburn and Wolves.' Forgive all this self congratulation by the Docklanders. But they were worthy of it and there were other observers with similar praise. Chairman Harold Needler and manager Cliff Britton of Hull went hoping to see Millwall beaten. That would have ensured Hull of the Third Division championship. They left with the title undecided and impressed with Millwall's masterly manner as they handed Walsall their second home defeat of the season. Then there was Dave Bowen, manager of Northampton, relegated from the First Division eyeing up the next season's opposition.

Walsall 1	Millwall 4	Referee: J. Finney (Hereford)
Middleton (pen)	*Julians (2)*	
	Dunphy	
	Brown	

Benny (Bells) Fenton is made manager of the month.

Eamon Dunphy (left) linked up well with Len Julians (right). Julians scored two important goals in this match. He was signed from Nottingham Forest and appeared 140 times, scoring 62 goals.

Walsall: Carling, Gregg, Sissons, Bennett, Harris, Harrison, Summers, Riley, Middleton, Satchwell, Taylor. Sub: Atthey.
Millwall: Stepney, Gilchrist, John, K. Jones, Snowdon, Wilson, Rowan, Julians, M. Brown, Dunphy, Neil.

Tottenham Hotspur v. Millwall

28 January 1967   FA Cup third round replay
White Hart Lane, London   Attendance: 58,189

The Lions went into this match on the back of two successive defeats, one of which was the Plymouth encounter that ended Millwall's unbeaten home League record of 59 games. As such, many Lions supporters feared the worst when the Spurs' FA Cup tie came around, especially with their star-studded team of internationals.

After a defiant goalless draw at The Den, in which Spurs had the better of things in front of 41,260 fans, Millwall would give a much better show in the replay, where some 5,000 fans would be locked out. However, this titanic struggle would go down in Lions history as another of Millwall's glorious failures, and it was summed up in the first two sentences of Brian James' report in the next day's *Daily Mail* when he stated:

'WITH the embarrassed gratitude of a millionaire who begged for a light, Spurs accepted from Millwall last night the simple goal they simply could not get for themselves. The goal that decided a game which had divided London surely as the Thames, came after two and a half hours of FA Cup football at its best.'

The goal thus described was the result of an appalling mistake by the normally dependable Tommy Wilson, a tall, sparse centre-back who had just nullified another Spurs attack in his own immaculate style, and, like the star performer milking the adulation, Tom laid the ball not to a colleague, but straight to Jimmy Greaves.

Greaves, lurking with intent, seized the opportunity to end Millwall's robust defiance, but miraculously he was denied but another Lions hero, goalkeeper Lawrie Leslie, who parried the Tottenham man's effort into the air only for the ball to drop to Alan Glizean to gleefully score the all-important goal, twenty minutes from time.

Tottenham, who would go on to win the cup that season, found this a game so incredibly hard to win, while Millwall – as in the first game – attempted nothing they could not achieve. Alan Willey was for a long time the Lions only attacker, but even with the limited assaults on the Tottenham goal, both Knowles and Kinnear were forced to make goal-line clearances, and Pat Jennings was drawn into two very good saves, as the roar of 'Millwall, Millwall' was heard all round this famous North London arena.

But it was Spurs who were creating the majority of the chances, with Greaves weaving his close dribbling magic, and on three occasions he worked his way into the Millwall area – only for three Leslie saves to leave the England man dancing in exasperation.

Tackles were flying in from every direction – some of which bordered on the downright dangerous – and Dunphy and Mackay, Julians and England, probably found it hard to exchange any pleasantries at the end. Leslie continued to paw away shots from Robertson, Venables, and Mackay in the first half, who, along with Cliff Jones and Gilzean, were thwarted in the second. In the end Millwall's heroic and magnificent resistance came to nothing, only the pride in taking on one of England's

---

Tottenham Hotspur 1   **Millwall 0**   **Referee:** D.W. Smith (Stonehouse)
Gilzean

Jimmy Greaves' flying header leaves Lawrie Leslie to look on.

best clubs to the limit in two games that attracted nearly 100,000 spectators between them.

'That was a hard one! Millwall must be certainties for promotion. The goal was a tragedy for them – they gave it to us on a plate.'
Bill Nicholson, Spurs manager

1966/67:

P	W	D	L	F	A	PTS
42	18	9	15	49	58	45

Second Division
Eighth Place
Manager: Benny Fenton
Top Goalscorer: Len Julian (17)
Average Attendance: 16,522

Tottenham Hotspur: Jennings, Kinnear, Knowles, Mullery, England, Mackay, Robertson, Greaves, Gilzean, Venables, Jones. Sub: Saul.
Millwall: Leslie, Gilchrist, Cripps, Jones, Snowdon, Wilson, Hunt, Willey, Julians, Dunphy, Neil. Sub: McCullough.

MILLWALL v. CRYSTAL PALACE

13 April 1968
The Den, London

Football League Division Two
Attendance: 14,782

This game ceased to be a competitive encounter after Ken Jones headed Millwall into the lead in the 21st minute from a Keith Weller corner. Millwall then took over and made it a nightmare for Palace – who were as poor as Millwall were good. This was Millwall in top gear and their football was fluid and pleasing to the eye, while individual talents were harnessed to the ethic of teamwork.

On the other hand Palace, who to their credit never gave up trying, were often caught in possession and this was coupled with their failure to control the ball on a hard pitch. It was a day they should forget quickly. The quick-moving Lions cruelly exposed the gambles made by Palace boss Bert Head. Full-back Eddie Presland was pressed into the centre half roll but came out second best to Bryan Conlon. Steve Kember was tried at centre forward, but his task proved virtually impossible against the tight marking of George Jacks.

Another plan instituted by Head that also backfired was the hapless Terry Long's task of shadowing Keith Weller – which proved to be the most damaging move of the afternoon. The former Spurs forward had a field day, his brilliant display of front running and ball control had the Palace defence at sixes and sevens.

Such was the form of Weller that general manager Benny Fenton told him to slow down and save himself for the other Easter games – although it was still Weller who caught the eye and earned himself a standing ovation at the end. Weller's team-mate Jacks won the praise of manager Fenton, who said 'Week after week, George is given a specific job to do and he does it with great distinction every time. Derby's Kevin Hector, Hill of Bolton, and Cardiff's Toshack, have all been played out of the game by him. Today he was told to mark Kember, and again he did his job superbly, for Kember had hardly a kick.'

Fenton also added 'the lads played well today, but I think they performed better the week before against Plymouth'. One of the main reasons for Millwall's excellent showing stemmed from the fact they were faster on and off the ball than Palace. 'We have a unique training scheme which speeds the players up. This is really beginning to show now,' claimed Fenton.

The best Palace effort, until Woodruff scored a consolation goal in the 87th minute, was supplied by Mark Lazarus with a twenty-yard shot that hit the cross bar and rebounded clear. Bryan Conlon scored on 38 and 72 minutes, another from Jones after 61 minutes, and a header from Derek Possee on 70 minutes gave Millwall their biggest win of the season and Palace their heaviest defeat.

Millwall 5
Jones (2)
Conlon (2)
Possee

Crystal Palace 1
Woodruff

Referee: H.G. New (Portsmouth)

Ken Jones who scored two goals in this match.

George Jacks who was praised by Benny Fenton for his work rate. Millwall signed him from Queens Park Rangers and he appeared in 161 games and was sub in 7 games scoring 9 goals.

1967/68:

P	W	D	L	F	A	PTS
42	14	17	11	62	50	45

Second Division
Seventh Place
Manager: Benny Fenton
Top Goal scorer: Keith Weller (14)
Highest attendance: QPR, 21,436

'Another local derby, which we all wanted desperately to win, and on the day we completely took control, and no one could have lived with us on the day. Team spirit was an essential part of our game.'
Billy Neil, Millwall FC

Millwall: King, Gilchrist, Cripps, Jones, Kitchener, Burnett, Possee, Weller, Conlon, Jacks, Neil. Sub: Plume.
Crystal Palace: Jackson, Sewell, Bannister, McCormick, Presland, Payne, Long, Lazarus, Kember, Woodruff, Tomkins. Sub: Vansittart.

Millwall v. Dundee

5 August 1968
The Den, London

Friendly
Attendance: 7,041

Millwall returned home to face Scottish First Division side Dundee after concluding a successful tour of Holland, where they defeated Go Ahead 2-0 and held Sparta Rotterdam to a 1-1 draw. To finalise their pre-season warm up the Lions supporters were entertained by an eight-goal gambol that provided a bright curtain-raiser at The Den, although manager Benny Fenton refused to get carried away with this masterful display and insisted on playing down the triumph. 'Don't get me wrong. I'm as pleased as anybody – with the way the lads played – and the way the goals were scored,' said Fenton, 'but we can't put too much emphasis on the result. We will have to face a lot stiffer opposition – it's a little to early to start celebrating.'

Despite Fenton's reservations, the game was a mighty good morale booster for the Lions. After the way they tore the Dundee defence to shreds they must have been confident of testing the best sides in the Second Division. Admittedly the Dundee side were always struggling to find their composure and gave little hint of the form that had earned them a good record against European opposition. They were especially shaky in defence, where the rearguard men dallied around like a bunch of unsure schoolboys.

But make no mistake about it, Millwall made plenty of openings – and took the chances with such deadly effect that Dundee's defensive frailties looked much worse than they were. Front line ace Keith Weller showed that he had wasted no time in getting into the form that made him a high price target for top clubs in the previous season.

The contrast from the last season was that Weller was getting proper support in attack, with Derek Possee tormenting the Scottish defenders, and Bryan Conlon looking the near-perfect middle man as he powered into the penalty box to threaten the Scots' goal.

It was also a night for the Millwall defenders, who were allowed some time to sweep upfield to boost the attack to form an eight-man barrage. Full-backs Harry Cripps and John Gilchrist regularly moved into Dundee territory to add more pressure on an already overworked defence.

With such overwhelming authority goals were bound to come – and once they scented the kill the Lions kept up the pressure with no let-up – even after a four-goal first half. Goals came as early as the 5th minute when Weller won a corner that Possee nodded home. Millwall went 2-0 up on 33 minutes after Stewart fouled Conlon in the area, for Weller to sidefoot the penalty into the corner of the net. Number three arrived after 38 minutes when a Weller-Jones move sent the ball through for Conlon to ram home from the edge of the area.

A minute before half-time Cripps raced up field to sling across a centre, which Possee headed home. The second half carried on in the same vein as the first, and after 66 minutes Conlon latched onto a through ball and capably turned pivot Easton inside-out, before netting number five. Barely two minutes later Weller cut in from the left wing to drive in a fierce shot to register the sixth.

The seventh arrived with sixteen minutes left, when Jones flicked a free kick into the air for Weller to volley into the net from 30 yards. The eighth and last goal came in the 77th minute when Possee's centre found Conlon, who slammed the ball home past a distraught Donaldson for his hat-trick.

Millwall 8
Weller (3)
Conlon (3)
Possee (2)

Dundee 0

Referee: G.F. Keep (London)

Left: Keith Weller was a front line ace and scorer of one of the hat-tricks. He was signed from Tottenham Hotspurs and played 135 games scoring 41 goals between 1967 and 1970. *Above right:* Derek Possee scored 2 goals and was very close to a hat-trick. He was also signed from Tottenham and played in 244 games between 1967 and 1973 scoring 87 goals. *Below right:* Brian Conlon the ideal centre forward scored a hat-trick. Having been signed from Darlington he appeard 44 times scoring 13 goals between 1967 and 1969.

The night could have been really rounded off if an earlier Derek Possee effort had not been disallowed – a decision which deprived the match of a hat-trick of hat-tricks.

1968/69:

P	W	D	L	F	A	PTS
42	17	9	16	57	49	43

Second Division
Tenth Place
Manager: Benny Fenton
Top Goalscorer: Bryan Conlon (16)
Highest Attendance: Crystal Palace 27,913

'This was one of the best individual performances from one player, namely Keith Weller – near perfection in everything he did. My old team-mate when I was playing in Scotland happened to be their goalkeeper (Ally Donaldson), and he said he was mesmerised by his display as well, luckily for him, he went off at half-time.'
Billy Neil, Millwall FC

Millwall: King, Gilchrist, Cripps, Jones, Kitchener, Burnett, Possee, Weller, Conlon, Jacks, Neil.
Dundee: Donaldson, Wilson, Houston, Murray, Easton, Stewart, Campbell, Duncan, Wilson, G McLean, J McLean.

CHARLTON ATHLETIC v. MILLWALL

10 August 1968   Football League Second Division
The Valley, London   Attendance: 27,504

To set the season off to a good start Millwall were given a local derby against Charlton – and what a curtain-raiser this pulsating encounter turned out to be. Millwall showed again their goal-scoring potential and promise for the season, but they were taken aback very early on as Charlton went ahead after two minutes.

Harry Gregory took a free kick that Matt Tees headed down for Keith Peacock to beat Bryan King from a couple of yards. This inspired the home team, who kept up a constant flow of attacks – which failed to breach the Lion's defence again. As Millwall began to settle, Wright had to come out to punch the ball off Derek Possee's head as the little winger came dashing in.

Denis Burnett, who had earlier brought down Gregory, was warned for a rash tackle on Treacy, before Millwall came back to equalise through a Bryan Conlon header in the 18th minute. It was then the Lions turn to take the lead from another header, this time from Possee, on the half hour. Keith Weller seemingly made the points safe as he made it 3-1 after 48 minutes with a terrific 20-yard drive.

But with Millwall still celebrating, Ray Treacy's 49th-minute strike reduced the arrears for Charlton. Tees was once more involved as he chested down a Bobby Curtis free kick for the Irishman to score. Three minutes later, however, Possee restored Millwall's two-goal advantage when he got a touch to Barry Kitchener's header from a Weller corner.

Still Charlton would not give in, and when Gregory scored with yet another headed goal for Charlton's third in the 75th minute, Millwall had to dig in with great resolve for the last quarter of an hour to hold on to what they had, as the game swung from end to end.

Keith Weller, Millwall's cockney wizard, went to hospital for a check-up on his injured ankle after his dominating role in the magnificent 4-3 victory over Charlton. Weller who was sold by Spurs to Millwall a year earlier, looked to be one of the best bargains in recent years. His thunder-bolt goal in the second half was equally as good as anything Bobby Charlton, Geoff Hurst, or Jimmy Greaves had ever scored. His corners and free kicks – struck purposely with the outside of the foot, with a vicious swerve into the danger zones – are just a part of his repertoire.

Charlton 3   Millwall 4   **Referee:** L. Callaghan (Merthyr Tydfil)
Peacock   *Conlon*
Gregory   *Possee (2)*
Treacy   *Weller*

Ken Jones in action during the match.

Only the injury marred a glittering display, which underlined that Millwall had only to play consistently to hop into the First Division. Apart from one petty foul on Millwall's George Jacks, the players of both sides made the game into a spectacle containing all the drama anyone could require. Charlton manager Eddie Firmani was quick to point out the defensive clangers, which Millwall took full advantage of, including the careless lapse by young Paul Went that set up Millwall's equaliser. Millwall boss Benny Fenton insisted, after a week in which his team had scored a dozen goals, that he was still interested in finding another striker. This was Millwall's first victory at The Valley since March 1933.

1968/69:

P	W	D	L	F	A	PTS
42	17	9	16	57	49	43

Second Division
Tenth Place
Manager: Benny Fenton
Top goal scorer: Keith Weller (16)
Highest Attendance: Crystal Palace 27,913

'Charlton games were always good to play in, great atmosphere, usually end to end stuff, and always close. When you have players like Weller and Possee up front you always felt you could win, potential match winners in their own right.'
Billy Neil, Millwall FC

Charlton Athletic: Wright, Curtis, Burkett, Campbell, Went, Reeves, Hince, Tees, Treacy, Gregory, Peacock, Sub Kinsey.
Millwall: King, Gilchrist, Cripps, Jones, Kitchener, Burnett, Possee, Weller, Conlon, Jacks, Neil, Sub Dunphy.

Millwall v. Preston North End

29 April 1972
The Den

Football League Second Division
Attendance: 19,123

Millwall's final game was at home to Preston, and if they won and Birmingham lost at Sheffield Wednesday, First Division football would be achieved at the Den for the first time ever. A crowd of nearly 20,000 came to see Millwall exact revenge on the side who had given the Lions their biggest defeat of the season.

The deadlock was broken when Derek Possee raced onto a Gordon Bolland pass to give Millwall the lead after 20 minutes on a glue pot pitch at the Den. But the Lions, needing both points to stand a chance of promotion, might have been five up in the first half-hour had they been more decisive in front of goal. Millwall scorned defence and pushed eight, sometimes nine, men up in the early stages, but good football was difficult on the muddy pitch. Millwall might well have scored twice in the first eight minutes, first Eamon Dunphy was left with a clear shot at goal after a centre from Gordon Bolland, but the Eire international drove wildly over the top. Then Brian Brown was left with an empty net in front of him after a cross from Doug Allder, but he struck the ball well wide, with Alan Kelly struggling to get back into position. Preston broke well from defence at times and Alex Spark shot over from close in, but it was Millwall who was making almost all the running. Kelly went full length to save from Allder as Millwall continued to press and were rewarded with a goal from Derek Possee in the 20th minute. Bolland pushed the ball through the middle, after it had been deflected by a defender, which left Possee with only Kelly to beat. For a moment, he appeared to have lost control, but as the goalkeeper came out, Possee recovered to drive the ball home.

Two minutes later, Millwall should have gone two up, when Barry Bridges broke clear, but Kelly got a hand to his shot although the ball trickled behind the goalkeeper, it went just wide. Millwall began to lose their early fire for, following their goal, they reverted to their usual tactics of nine men back with only Possee and Bridges left up field. This enabled Preston to come into the game. A bad back pass from John McMahon almost allowed Allder to break through, but Kelly came out to avert the danger. Allder shot wide in another promising attack, but nearing the interval the game went flat with very few exciting moments. Possee was kicked on his right leg two minutes after the break, but battled on without treatment. Within a minute, he had a chance to put Millwall further ahead, but his close range shot was blocked as two Preston defender's converged on him.

Millwall seemed frightened of Preston snatching an equaliser and were still too cautious, though they continued to attack strongly at times. Dunphy played through some neat passes, but the muddy conditions often gave the Millwall strikers just as many problems as the Preston defence. The prominent Allder tried to slip through on the left flank but McMahon came racing back to concede a corner. Millwall skipper Dennis Burnett then took a free kick near the half-way line, which resulted in Kelly going full length to save a header from Bolland. Millwall still looked shaky when Preston moved up mainly due to anxiety. Yet, the Lions continued to carve out the best chances and after Bolland had been tripped by Hawkins just outside the Preston box, the visitors were again in trouble. Dunphy flicked the free kick to Bolland whose powerful drive had Kelly beaten, but went just wide. The tension was finally lifted when Dougie Allder sent over yet another inch perfect cross for Bridges to score Millwall's second from close range in the 72nd minute.

The rumour spread round the crowd that Birmingham were losing and by the end of

---

Millwall 2
Possee
Bridges

Preston North End 0

Referee: J. Hunting (Leicester)

Left: Doug Allder made inch perfect crosses in this match. He came through the youth team and reserves and signed in 1969. He played 215 games and 12 sub games scoring 13 goals – 1969-1975. *Right:* Barry Bridges settled the game from close range. He was signed from QPR and made 82 appearances for Millwall scoring 27 goals between 1970 and 1972. He also made 4 appearances for England.

the game the crowd was on the pitch perimeter waiting to swarm on the pitch at the final whistle, jubilant that Birmingham had blown it. Millwall players, shirts ripped from their backs, were onto the shoulders of the cheering crowd. The pitch had become an Ocean of Blue and White scarfs, fans singing, laughing and openly crying, bathing in a pool of unashamed emotion. Players who made the dressing room were toasting Division One. Suddenly there was an urgent message from the tannoy. There had been a dreadful mistake. Birmingham had won at Hillsborough. It took five, maybe ten seconds for the horrific news to sink in and a hush swept the ground. As the supporters left the ground, they knew Birmingham needed a single point from their final game at Orient to rob Millwall of what, so it seemed, had briefly been theirs. Millwall's fate was decided at Brisbane Road when Birmingham beat Orient in front of a crowd of 33,000. 8,000 of this crowd were Millwall supporters who had gone to cheer on the Orient.

1971/72:

P	W	D	L	F	A	PTS
42	19	17	6	64	46	55

Second Division
Third Place
Manager: Benny Fenton
Top Goalscorer: Derek Possee (15)
Highest Attendance: QPR, 24,266
Average Attendance: 16,262

Millwall: King, Brown, Cripps, Dorney, Kitchener, Burnett, Possee, Bolland, Bridges, Dunphy, Allder, sub: Smethurst.
Preston North End: Kelly, McMahon, Ross, Bird, Hawkins, Spark, Heppolette, Lyall, Tarbuck, Young, Lamb, sub: Wilson.

EVERTON v. MILLWALL

3 February 1973
Goodison Park, Liverpool

FA Cup fourth round
Attendance: 32,277

After missing out on promotion the previous season and sitting in the lower half of the table in mid term, something special was needed to revitalise Millwall's fortunes and the perfect tonic was an intriguing FA Cup tie up on Merseyside.

Millwall had beaten Newport County in the previous round, and now the Lions were paired with Everton of the First Division. The Lions had just sold Derek Possee and their firepower now relied on the exploits of new signing Alf Wood and Gordon Bolland. Millwall being the underdogs, many onlookers thought it was just a formality that Harry Catterick's Everton would progress as a matter of course, but a big shock was on the way for many who dismissed Millwall (who hadn't won an away tie in this competition since 1951).

After a goal-less first half, in which Everton had thrown everything at Millwall including the kitchen sink, it was the Lions who incredibly took the lead from a free kick, which was added to by a second goal two minutes from time.

While Millwall swept triumphantly into the fifth round of the cup, Everton suffered abuse from the fans who hurled cushions on the pitch in disgust as the hero of the Old Kent Road, Harry Cripps – the most popular Lion at The Den – scored the vital first goal and then cleared an Everton shot off the line.

Millwall collected two bookings, Barry Kitchener and Bryan Brown, and conceded 30 free kicks for fouls. Love them or hate them, Millwall's tactics were successful on the day when Everton's own shortcomings in allowing themselves to be intimidated by Millwall's muscular they-shall-not-pass approach, which ultimately led to their downfall.

Everton's 11 fouls, plus some offside awards, meant that the game was punctuated by a free kick every two minutes, which may account for Benny Fenton's men playing for 40 minutes before they got within shooting distance of goalkeeper David Lawson. His Lions counterpart Bryan King was in constant demand. The first of a string of superb saves, and probably the best, came from Mick Buckley's pinpoint centre onto Joe Harper's forehead, but somehow King parried the header at point blank range, only to tip Harper's next effort over the bar as the Scot followed up.

The game started to become a contest in the football sense soon after the interval, but not before Bryan Brown had picked up a booking for a clattering Connolly. Soon after Harper did have the ball in the Millwall net (after 58 minutes of play) only to be rightly ruled offside.

Then, with half an hour to go, Mike Bernard's frustration got the better of him and fell hook line and sinker into the trap of retaliating to Millwall's tactics, felling Denis Burnett as he raced for goal some twenty yards out. Steve Brown took the free kick and burly left-back Cripps rose above a mass of heads to nod the ball down past Lawson.

Just before the kick was taken, Everton skipper Howard Kendall limped off to be replaced by Gary Jones, who joined in the Toffees' desperate efforts to draw level. With five minutes to go Jones had the chance to score: with King beaten, Cripps' burly frame came to the Lions' rescue as he blocked the shot on the line. Then, two minutes from time, Gordon Bolland set up one of the biggest cup upsets when he left the weary Everton defence in his wake, and centred for Alf Wood to head a spectacular second goal and send the home fans scurrying away in disgust for the exits.

Everton 0	Millwall 2	Referee: Harold Hackney (Barnsley)
	Cripps	
	Wood	

Millwall celebrate their 2-0 win over Everton in the FA Cup.

Harry Cripps said after the game. 'After beating Everton we deserve to dodge the big boys in the next round. We'll be happy to take on a team like Leeds at Wembley. The win at Everton is a big boost for the entire staff at Millwall. We haven't been having any luck and this result almost makes up for us missing promotion by a point last season. I'm told the last time we defeated Everton was in 1903 by a 1-0 score line, and that year we reached the semi-final.'

1972/73:

P	W	D	L	F	A	PTS
42	16	10	16	55	47	42

Second Division
Eleventh Place
Manager: Benny Fenton
Top Goalscorer: Gordon Bolland (19)
Highest Attendance: QPR, 16,136

Everton: Lawson, Wright, Style, Kendall, Kenyon, Hurst, Harper, Bernard, Belfitt, Buckley, Connolly. Sub: Jones.
Millwall: King, B. Brown, Cripps, Dorney, Kitchener, Burnett, S. Brown, Bolland, Wood, Dunphy, Allder, Sub; Saul.

MILLWALL v. FULHAM

20 January 1974   Football League Second Division
The Den, London   Attendance: 15,143

Millwall had their biggest gate of the season for the first ever Sunday Football League fixture against Fulham, and used this high profile game to ease out of the relegation zone through an early strike from Brian Clark. Indeed it was an honour to bestow upon one of the games' gentleman, for no one can take away his record of scoring such a historic goal – the first Sunday strike in the history of British League football.

The gate of 15,143 was high, but as a local derby it may not have been a real test for the popularity of professional soccer on Sunday. Fulham, who hadn't lost to the Lions in the previous four matches, were almost presented with a goal in the opening minute by the usually sound Alan Dorney (whose form hadn't been quite up to his best in the previous few matches). The mistake took the form of a misplaced back-pass to Bryan King which nearly let in Fulham's Les Barrett. The forward lost the chance capitalise when King dashed out of his goal to beat him to the ball. Following this narrow squeak it was the home side who went into the lead in the fourth minute.

Doug Allder, who had a good game, burst down the left wing and crossed the ball into the centre. Fulham centre-back John Lacy headed his clearance straight to Clark, who controlled the ball on his chest and let it drop before firing a right-foot volley into Mellor's net.

This goal made Fulham come at Millwall, with full-back Les Strong taking over a Terry Cooper role, in which one of his runs took him deep into the Millwall area for him to unleash a shot which King was happy to turn away for a corner.

Gordon Hill, who didn't always play an unorthodox game, was put in the clear by Allder's pass, but his bullet shot was in vain as it was beaten down by Peter Mellor – although more significantly Hill had been adjudged offside. It was sometimes said that at times the youngster was guilty of playing more for himself rather than the team.

The Lions were lucky to get away with a blatant foul in the box, Barry Lloyd was through and getting ready to get a shot at away when Dorney brought him down, but the referee waved play on amid protests from the Fulham players. Then Alan Slough broke down the right wing after beating his marker, played a one-two with Barrett and crossed the ball right on the goal line – but Barrett failed (by a whisker) to get a touch.

In Millwall's next foray Alf Wood did manage to get the ball into the net from a Gordon Bolland free kick but he quite obviously punched it in and the score was correctly disallowed. Hill was just wide with another scorcher, which came from an Allder corner after Alan Mullery had kicked the ball out.

A fierce shot by Bolland after Hill and Clark had set up a chance whistled inches over the bar, and when Hill, back helping out in defence, made a hash of a back pass, Fulham's Barrett was on to it like a flash before the combined efforts of a clutch of Lions defenders prevented him getting in a shot.

Clark then hit an upright in a brief Lion's attack, as Fulham were getting more into the game, but the home full-backs, alongside centre half Barry Kitchener, stuck to their jobs, with Dorney now recovering his poise to keep King from being troubled too often.

Eddie Jones had to concede a corner to prevent a Strong centre going to the menacing Barrett, but King took the ball cleanly from the corner kick, despite being under a great deal of pressure.

A lull in the play allowed an announcement to be made over the loudspeaker that

---

Millwall 1   **Fulham 0**   **Referee:** G.C. Kew (Amersham)
Clark

brought light relief and howls of laughter. It stated 'Will Mr Spike please return with keys to the Red Cow public house, we are waiting to open the pub'. Mr Spike was obviously enjoying the game too much to leave, for a repeat announcement was made at half-time.

King had to be at his best again for Millwall when he took the ball from Barrett after the dashing Fulham winger had made a belligerent run from his own area. Yet another dangerous centre from Strong came across but his forwards once more failed to take advantage of it when all the ball needed was the slightest of touches to produce the equaliser.

King then made a rare mistake three minutes into the second half when he dropped a ball from Lloyd. Jimmy Conway lobbed it towards the goal only for Kitchener to race back and head it out. The ball-dropping disease seemed to be catching, as Peter Mellor also erred at the other end, but Wood was unable to get up enough steam to get to this chance.

King had more to do in the second half, saving from Busby and Conway, but neither shot carried enough sting to trouble him. Hill caused Wood to shake his fist at him when he careered from the right wing over to the left to get into a shooting position, but the opportunity was lost and it was obvious that Wood had been in a better position to score.

The Millwall 'keeper saved his side a point when with a sheer reflex save he turned away an angled shot from Barrett, as Fulham went all out for the equaliser. Bad finishing prevented them from getting back on terms. They were, however, also fortunate not to concede another goal when Strong cleared off the line from Clark. After the game, Fulham manager Alec Stock stated, 'The game's all about getting the ball into the back of the net – and we didn't do that'.

1973/74:

P	W	D	L	F	A	PTS
42	14	14	14	51	51	42

Second Division
Twelfth Place
Manager: Benny Fenton.
Top Goalscorer: Alf Wood (21)
Average Attendance: 9,515.

MILLWALL FULHAM

FOOTBALL LEAGUE DIVISION TWO
SUNDAY 20 JANUARY 1974 KICK OFF 11.30 AM

Admission will be afforded free to anyone who has purchased this official Programme which will only be available at the Turnstiles

Millwall: King, Donaldson, Jones, Dorney, Kitchener, Allder, Bolland, Clark, Wood, Smethurst, Hill.

Fulham: Mellor, Fraser, Strong, Mullery, Lacy, Dunne, Conway, Slough, Busby, Lloyd, Barrett.

MILLWALL v. BRADFORD CITY

23 February 1985
The Den, London

Canon League Division Three
Attendance: 9,011

The Lions were on a roll after winning their last five games, which included victories over Chelsea and Leicester City in the FA Cup, then Newport County at home and Wigan away in the League, proceeded two days earlier by a Freight Rover Trophy win at Southend.

Millwall treated their biggest League crowd of the season to a 4-0 drubbing of the runaway Third Division leaders, for whom this was only their second defeat in 22 League matches. Again it was John Fashanu who was the Lions hero and his presence made it a very uncomfortable afternoon for the City. Fashanu capped a fine individual performance with two cracking goals.

Delighted Lions boss George Graham said 'I thought we started slowly in the first half, but in the second we played as well as we've done all season'. Former Leeds star Trevor Cherry, the Bradford boss, said, 'Millwall are a good side. We were never in with a chance and it's the worst we've played this season.' Graham explained, 'It's all down to hard work by the players and coaching staff and excellent team spirit.'

Skipper Les Briley, back after a two-match ban, showed his class after 28 minutes, when he received a quick throw-in from Steve Lovell, dribbled into the City area with some ease, then drew stand in City 'keeper Dave Harvey, before selflessly laying the ball back to Steve Lowndes, who stroked it home.

This set up the Lions for a storming second half, and if that piece of Briley class was something to behold then the next Millwall goal was of equally high quality, when Welsh international Lowndes chased Cusack's punt upfield. It seemed to be a hopeless task but he got to the ball and crossed for Fashanu to score with a soaring header from a near impossible angle.

Two late goals from the Lions emphasised their superiority. It was Fashanu who put the cherry on the cake with his second goal in the 80th minute. It was left to Yorkshireman David Cusack to finish off City and complete the scoring five minutes later.

1984/85:

P	W	D	L	F	A	PTS
46	26	12	8	73	42	90

Third Division
Second Place
Manager: George Graham
Top Goalscorer: Steve Lovell (21)
Highest Attendance: Leicester City FA Cup fifth round 16,160
Average Attendance: 6,442

'At the moment, I am doing things Rummenigge would be pleased with.'
John Fashanu

Millwall 4
Fashanu (2)
Lowndes
Cusack

Bradford City 0

Referee: T.D. Spencer (Salisbury)

Steve Lowndes scored the first of the four goals against Bradford City. He was signed from Newport County and appeared 119 times scoring 18 goals between 1983 and 1986.

Millwall: Sansome, Stevens, Hinshelwood, Briley, Nutton, Cusack, Lowndes, Fashanu, Chatterton, Lovell (Bremner), Otulaskowski.
Bradford City: Harvey, Clegg, With, McCall, Jackson, Evans, Hendrie (Holmes), Goodman, Campbell, Abbott, Ellis.

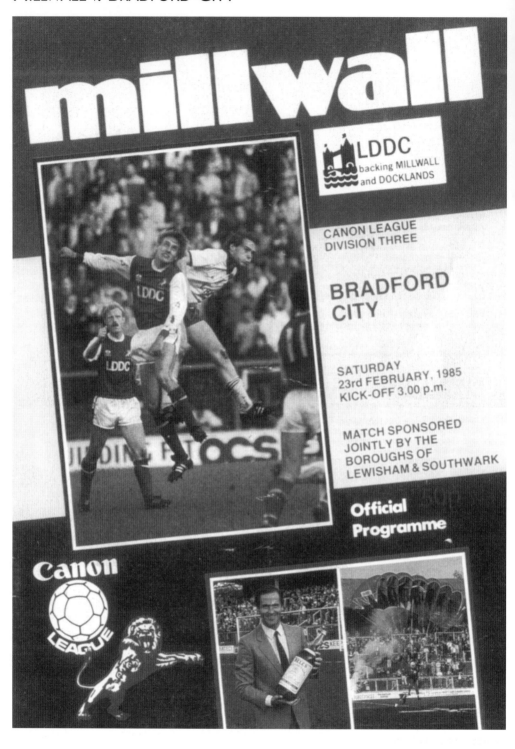

Theo Foley (left), Kevin Bremner (middle) and Les Briley (right) celebrate with a drop of champagne.

John Fashanu, the two-goal hero, was signed from Lincoln and played 65 games for Millwall scoring 19 goals between 1984 and 1986.

MILLWALL v. QUEENS PARK RANGERS

1 October 1988
The Den

Barclays League Division One
Attendance: 14,103

Many people said Millwall did not belong in the First Division. Many more said they could not possibly survive. But after a richly deserved victory, Millwall were top of the First Division for the first time in their 103 year history. Millwall's reputation – the intimidating Den, the uncompromising approach of their play – went before them and Rangers started with a huge inferiority complex. Millwall were hardly out of the Rangers half in the opening ten minutes until Lawrence, challenged heavily by Dennis, stood up after lengthy treatment to tap a free kick to Hurlock. He floated in a perfect cross for Cascarino to lose his marker and send a header past Nicky Johns. Almost immediately, Lawrence limped out, to be replaced by Jimmy Carter. The change threw Millwall out of their stride only temporarily, but it was enough to enable Rangers to catch their breath and score from their first genuine attack. Stein and Brock combined to find Francis on the edge of the area, and his instant turn and shot past Horne were reminiscent of the peak of his career. Any hopes Rangers may have had of then dictating the game were dispelled in three minutes through the inspiration of Terry Hurlock. He epitomises the Millwall style and like the team, it is one you either love or loathe. For the Millwall fans, Hurlock could do no wrong, and he enhanced his reputation by seizing on Brock's back pass after 35 minutes, drawing Johns and slipping the ball to Cascarino, who tapped his eighth goal of the season into the empty net. Two minutes later, Hurlock dispossessed Brock 30 yards out, and crashed an unstoppable shot past Johns. As Millwall rampaged forward, only a questionable offside decision robbed Cascarino of a third goal before half-time. To their credit, Rangers regrouped well, but Francis's disputed 67th minute penalty, awarded for Hurlock's challenge on Stein, was brilliantly saved by Horne. Allen's drive from the edge of the area gave the final scoreline a closer look than Ranger's warranted.

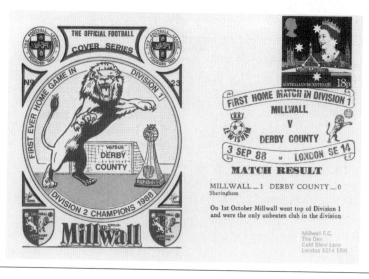

Millwall 3
Cascarino (2)
Hurlock

Queens Park Rangers 2
Francis
Allen

Referee: R. Lewis (Great Bookham)

Tony Cascarino (left) opens the scoring in the derby against Queens Park Rangers, at the Den with a header off Terry Hurlock's free kick. Tony Cascarino is also in the right-hand picture.

1988/89:

P	W	D	L	F	A	PTS
38	14	11	13	47	52	53

First Division
Tenth Place
Manager: John Docherty
Top Goalscorer: Tony Cascarino (24)
Highest Attendance: Liverpool 22,126
Average Attendance: 15,416

Millwall: Horne, Stevens, Dawes, Hurlock, Wood, McLeary, Lawrence (Carter), Morgan, Sheringham, Cascarino, O'Callaghan.
Queens Park Rangers: Johns, Kerslake, Dennis (Falco), Parker, McDonald, Maguire, Allen, Francis, Fereday, Stein, Brock (Barker).

MILLWALL v. SHEFFIELD WEDNESDAY

27 October 1990
The Den

Barclays League Division Two
Attendance: 12,863

Millwall came back from the dead to destroy Sheffield Wednesday's unbeaten record with a display that Lions manager Bruce Rioch described as 'stupendous'. After he saw a four-goal second-half comeback, Rioch said, 'it was like an exhilarating cup tie'. To come back from two down against an excellent footballing side is brilliant. 'We took some punishment, we expected to, but the players then went out and did really well'. With both sides strongly fancied in the promotion race, victory was vital both for points and morale, and for fifty minutes it seemed that Wednesday would comfortably emerge with their sixth away win of the season. They had the midfield completely sewn up thanks to international stars John Sheridan and Danny Wilson. Two goals in three minutes from the prolific David Hirst, his 10th and 11th of the season, put Millwall in disarray, only the woodwork saved them from being 4-0 down by the interval. But then fate played a hand. Wednesday's Swedish international Roland Nilsson suffered a serious knee injury and was carried off. There was also the enforced departure of captain Nigel Pearson who was replaced by ex-Millwall player Lawrie Madden. Wednesday's composure was shattered. Cheered on by the biggest crowd of the season, Millwall subjected Wednesday to incessant pressure. When Jimmy Carter volleyed home from a Kevin O'Callaghan free-kick, which found him running in at the far post, it was merely a hint of things to come. Jimmy Carter then weaved into the box to pull back for Teddy Sheringham to grabbed his 10th of the season and the equaliser. What happened next was one of those heart-stopping moments of high drama which Millwall fans will talk about for as long as the pubs in The Old Kent Road serve beer. In what seemed like slow motion Welsh international Malcolm Allen ignored the two teammates on his right, cut past Peter Shirtliff and slid his shot under Wednesday's keeper Kevin Pressman. 'I suppose it was instinct, but I hadn't scored for seven games and went out onto the pitch knowing I had to be positive,' said Allen. 'It's got to be my most valuable goal for a long time. And our comeback was the best I've ever been involved in.' Finally, in a furious last five minutes Alex Rae scored the fourth in injury time and clinched victory. 'They have done Millwall proud' said Rioch. 'This was a great advertisement for football'.

1990/91:

P	W	D	L	F	A	PTS
46	20	13	13	70	51	73

Second Division
Fifth Place
Manager: Bruce Rioch
Top Goalscorer: Teddy Sheringham (33)
Highest Attendance: West Ham United, 20,591
Average Attendance: 10,846

Millwall 4
Carter
Sheringham
Allen, Rae

Sheffield Wednesday 2
Hirst (2)

Referee: B. Hill (Kettering).

Teddy Sheringham gets the equaliser to make it 2-2 chased by Malcolm Allen who got the third.

Gary Waddock outjumps England's Carlton Palmer in midfield.

Wednesday try to keep a hold of Alex Rae but he still manages to score the fourth goal.

Millwall: Brannigan, Stevens, Dawes, Waddock, Wood, McLeary, Carter, Allen, Sheringham, Rae, O'Callaghan. Subs: Stephenson, McCarthy.
Sheffield Wednesday: Pressman, Nilsson, King, Palmer, Shirtliff, Pearson, Wilson, Sheridan, Hirst, Williams, Worthington, Subs: Francis, Maddon.

Millwall v. Sheffield Wednesday

26 January 1991   FA Cup fourth round
The Den   Attendance: 13,653

This was Millwall's second meeting with Sheffield Wednesday after their goal feast in the League. The fans were expecting another high scoring game and they were not dismayed with this 8 goal thriller in the FA Cup fourth round. Rae's last gasp equaliser in this epic 4-4 draw had the twenty-one year old Scots man enthusing, 'That was a great game to be involved in and even better to score my second goal so late on. To be fair Sheffield Wednesday are a First Division team and they have some very good players. But we gave a really great battling performance and kept on at them until the final minute. I think we showed real commitment and spirit'. Even the power cut at half-time with the stands in darkness and floodlights at half power could not dim this electrifying thriller of a cup tie. O'Callaghan, a late replacement for the injured Les Briley, was in a different class and instigated most of Millwall's attacks, in the first half particularly. But it was fellow winger Paul Stephenson who gave the Lions a dream start after just 57 seconds when he drove home after the Wednesday defence failed to clear Teddy Sheringham's over head kick. The die had been cast for a classic and the following 89 minutes followed suit. Although Millwall, lead by the superb Sheringham, were lethal up front, their defence were in disarray at the back. Time after time the central pairing of Steve Wood and Alan McLeary, failed to clear even the simplest of chances. And when they did, it was either straight to a Sheffield player or hopelessly out of reach of a team-mate. Marking at set pieces was just as catastrophic and all four Sheffield goals were a direct result of poor defending. The first of these came after twelve minutes when, Nigel Pearson's free kick was flicked on by Viv Anderson for John Harkes. The American cut into the box, slipped a neat pass to David Hirst who dragged the ball back before

firing past Brian Horne. That in itself should have been warning enough, but the Lions fell into the same trap again on thirty minutes when John Sheridan's free kick found Pearson eighteen yards out. Pearson's shot was parried by Horne and the unmarked Trevor Francis simply nodded home at the far post. But Millwall's tremendous battling instincts spurred them on again and Rae finished off a neat three-man move started by O'Callaghan to level. Then O'Callaghan curled a twenty-five-yard free kick inches over the bar and then laid on a great chance for John Goodman which he blasted over – the pendulum finally looked to be swinging Millwall's way. But in a game that never ceased to amaze, it was Ron Atkinson's side who drew blood next, Sheridan's free kick headed on by Harkes for Pearson to slot home after fifty-five minutes. 3-2 to Sheffield. Three minutes later and, surprise surprise, the Lions

Teddy Sheringham celebrates his equaliser during our FA Cup third round victory over Leicester

---

Millwall 4   **Sheffield Wednesday 4**   **Referee:** R F Nixon (Wirral)

Stephenson   *Pearson*
Rae (2)   *Hirst,, Francis*
Sheringham   *Anderson*

Paul Stephenson (right) gave the Lions a dream start after scoring in the first minute when Wednesday failed to clear a loose ball. Paul is seen here being congratulated by Alex Rae, who would go on to score twice during the course of the game.

levelled again! John Goodman's astonishing pace saw him accelerate past the flat-footed Anderson and play a perfect pass for Sheringham to nonchalantly flick home his 20th goal of the season. You barely dared blink for missing another goal and Keith Stevens nearly obliged when he mishit a 75th-minute clearance straight into Hirst's path. Luckily, Horne was on hand to tip Hirst's shot round the post for a corner. Five minutes later another Wednesday corner looked certain to have written the final chapter, when full-back Anderson planted a firm header into the roof of the net. Relentless Lion's pressure paid off when Rae stabbed home a Sheringham cross with barely fifteen seconds left on the clock. 'To score 4 goals at home and not win you would normally be disappointed,' said Lion's boss Bruce Rioch. 'But if I said I was it would be taking away from my players, who gave their all. It was a fantastic game from the first minute to the last and would have been a shame if either team had lost today.'

1990/91: FA Cup

3   5 Jan   (h) Leicester City W 2-1   10,766
Horne, Stevens, Dawes, Waddock, Wood, McLeary, Stephenson, Goodman, Sheringham, Rae, O'Callaghan.
4R 30 Jan   (a) Sheffield Wed L 0-2   25,140
Horne, Stevens, Dawes, Waddock, Wood, McLeary, Stephenson, Goodman, Sheringham, Rae, O'Callaghan.

Millwall: Horne, Stevens, Dawes, Waddock, Wood, McLeary, Stephenson, Goodman, Sheringham, Rae, O'Callaghan
Sheffield Wednesday: Turner, Anderson, King, Palmer, Shirtliff, Pearson, Francis (Williams), Sheridan, Hirst, Harkes, Worthington.

Millwall v. Sporting Lisbon

4 August 1993
The New London Stadium

The Opening of the Stadium
Attendance: 17,887

After eighty-three years, Millwall moved 200 yards up Mercury Way to a Magnificent Stadium built by Tilbury Douglas that seated 20,000 supporters. It took 59 weeks to build at a cost of £15.5 million. With no fences and no segregation, there were 32 executive boxes, an 800-seat restaurant, 17 refreshment outlets and television monitors. It was also built to hold pop concerts and boxing tournaments. There was a big build-up for the opening, with the late Leading Labour Party minister Rt Hon. John Smith QC cutting the ribbon for the Millwall fans to watch their football in luxury. Little did they know that within five years the club would have to call in the receivers with the soaring costs for success. Bobby Robson brought his star-studded side for a spectacular football occasion in the history of the club. Seventeen-year-old Ben Thatcher was making his debut, John Kerr and Malcolm Allen were paired up front in the absence of Jon Goodman and Jamie

Moralee. Millwall took the lead through Canadian John Kerr, when he slotted Ian Dawes' cross past the Lisbon goalkeeper in the sixteenth minute. He went down in history as the first person to score at The New Den. However, within three minutes Sporting were level after Bulgarian international Krassimire Balakov was brought down in the box by Tony McCarthy. Balakov took the penalty which Kasey Keller stopped superbly, only to see leading goalscorer Jorge Cadete fire in the rebound. The party celebrations were ruined by a late goal. The Portuguese side won the game with an 87th-minute strike from Polish star Andrzej Juskowiak.

Millwall chairman said after the game. 'It is without doubt the finest stadium in the country. It may not be the biggest, but it is the best and we are after the sort of business Wembley gets.' Millwall finished the season third in the Endsleigh League Division One only to lose to Derby County in the play-offs.

1993/94:

P	W	D	L	F	A	PTS
46	19	17	10	58	49	74

Division: One
Third Place
Manager: Mick McCarthy
Top Goalscorer: Alex Rae
Highest Attendance: Arsenal FA Cup 20,093
Average Attendance: 9,811

Millwall 1
Kerr

Sporting Lisbon 2
Cadete
Juskowiaka

Referee: John Moules

Aerial view of the new stadium.

Aerial view of the first goal scored at the New Den by John Kerr.

Millwall: Keller (Emberson), Cunningham (Huxford 73), Dawes, Maguire, T. McCarthy (Thatcher 73), Stevens, Roberts, Bogie, Allen (Dolby 73), Kerr (Murray 71), Luscombe (Verveer 71).
Sporting Lisbon: Lemajic, Nelson (Juskowiaka), Peixe, Valckx, Torres, Sousa, Figo (Capucho 73), Balacov, Pacheco (Vujavic 57), Cadete, Filipe.

Arsenal v. Millwall

18 January 1995   FA Cup third round replay
Highbury, London   Attendance: 32,319

Millwall plunged Arsenal and George Graham into further crisis with a dramatic FA Cup victory. Goals from Mark Beard and Mark Kennedy topped and tailed Millwall's celebrations in the third-round replay, putting former Millwall manager Graham under pressure to resign.

The victory took Millwall into a glamorous tie against Chelsea in the next round. Jubilant manager Mick McCarthy said 'This means another £300,000 in the pot for us. The chairman is already saying we have to draw with Chelsea at home and then beat them away. I think we played better on the night and created more chances than they did. I told my players it was not good enough to draw at home and I thought they played through them and around them.'

This was a fierce Highbury battle of the sort Arsenal used to thrive on – and the sort they rarely lost. However, they stumbled and fell against a Millwall side that were simply the better team on the night. The Division One team deserved to go through into the next round. Millwall weren't a team of superstars, but they had some good young players and they knew how to cope in a battle.

The Gunners played with plenty of heart, but they didn't have the know-how or the ability to unlock a defence. Keith Stevens, nicknamed Rhino, stood firm and Arsenal could find no way past. Instead it was young men like Mark Beard and Mark Kennedy who caught the eye. Kennedy, a Republic of Ireland Under-21 international, particularly tormented Arsenal.

The home team didn't have a single player to trouble Millwall. In Ian Wright they had a man who can cause damage, but, on a night of bitter defeat, Wright grabbed the attention for the wrong reasons when he was involved in a late incident with Millwall's Alex Rae and was also booked for the 12th time that season when he crashed into Kasey Keller.

Millwall had already signalled that a mauling was on the cards when they grabbed their opener after ten minutes. Jason Van Blerk played a one-two with Dave Mitchell, Van Blerk's subsequent cross picking out the twenty-year-old Beard waiting at the far post. The striker produced a neat finish to beat Seaman. The dangerous Kevin Campbell forced Keller

Mark Beard scores past Seaman at the far post.

Arsenal 0   **Millwall 2**   **Referee:** S. Lodge (Barnsley).
                         Beard
                         Kennedy

Ian Wright's late challenge on Keller is more than Rhino can stand, as he and Jason van Blerk guide him away.

into a superb save and was again foiled by the American in the second half. Keller then stopped an Andy Linighan header. Despite these flurries, Arsenal created too little, with their best chance falling to substitute Tony Adams six minutes from time, but he shot hopelessly wide. Millwall might have scored again before the interval when another of their Australian contingent, Alistair Edwards, broke clear in the 35th minute only to shoot over the bar.

Arsenal fans will argue that Keller should have been sent off when his momentum carried himself and the ball outside of the area after taking a clean catch, but referee Lodge merely showed him a yellow card.

Millwall kept pushing forward and sealed victory in the final minute when Kennedy, racing onto a long clearance, was being begged by supporters and team-mates to take the ball into the corner to eat up some precious time. Young Mark had other ideas, however, and capped a brilliant evening for Lions of all ages when he cracked home a stunning decider past a startled Seaman.

1994/95:

P	W	D	L	F	A	PTS
46	16	14	16	60	60	62

First Division
Twelfth Place
Manager: Mick McCarthy
Top Goalscorer: Alex Rae (10)
Highest Attendance: Chelsea FA Cup fourth round 18,573
Average Attendance: 7,679

Arsenal: Seaman, Dixon, Winterburn Linighan, Keown, Jensen, Hillier, Morrow, Parlour, Campbell, Wright, Subs: Adams, Bartram, Flatts.
Millwall: Keller, Dawes, Van Blerk, Roberts, Witter, Stevens, Beard, Rae, Edwards, Mitchell, Kennedy. Subs: Webber, T. Carter, Savage.

WALSALL v. MILLWALL

16 March 1999
Bescot Stadium

Auto Windscreens Shield Southern Area Final Second Leg
Attendance: 9,158

Joint managers Keith Stevens and Alan McLeary had now achieved a dream for all the Millwall followers, a trip to the Twin Towers of Wembley. The Lions had just made it before the demolition of the famous stadium and fans would have a tale to tell their grandchildren when they saw their team play on the hallowed turf. But it wasn't all plain sailing. On the way at Bournemouth, after drawing 1-1 Millwall went through on penalties winning 4-3. Then, after 90 minutes at The Den against Gillingham with the score 0-0, Richard Sadlier scored the golden goal to put Millwall through to the final against Walsall. The first leg was played at The Den, and Millwall won by one goal to nil, scored by Tim Cahill after just three minutes. It was all or nothing in the second leg with 2,000 Millwall supporters making the trip to the Midlands.

Right from the start The Lions took the game to their opponents and carved out chances in a surprisingly open game. Neil Harris and Ricky Newman both had efforts narrowly off-target, whilst Paul Ifill was tying Neil Pointon in knots on the right flank. At the other end the defence looked assured with Ben Roberts, who had needed a fitness test on a badly bruised foot, saving a low drive from Colin Cramb and Joe Dolan making a brilliant tackle to stop the progress of Cramb. Bobby Bowry and Ricky Newman, meanwhile, worked tirelessly in midfield, fetching and carrying, covering and hustling to cut off the supply line to Wrack, Cramb and Brissett.

Having weathered a brief Walsall storm mid-way through the first half, during which Brissett fired over the bar, Millwall began to get a foot hold. Just before the half-hour, Neil Harris forced James Walker to make a finger-tip save, but the impressive Saddlers keeper was about to be beaten. In the 36th minute, Paul Ifill and Neil Harris worked the ball to Richard Sadlier, who thumped it into the top corner of the net at the second attempt. There was no temptation to sit on that lead, as Ricky Newman with a block-tackle-cum-shot forced Walker to make a stunning save before the 'keeper was also tested by Harris and Lucas Neill.

In the second half, Darren Wrack burst through the Lions rearguard for the first time. However, Ben Roberts spotted the danger and was off his line in a flash to deny the winner. Thereafter, until the final minutes, Walsall's raids became sporadic and Millwall carved out chance upon chance to put the result beyond doubt. The best of these certainly fell to Neil Harris on the hour, when great work from Paul Ifill put him away. The Lions top scorer kept his cool to round the 'keeper, but slightly off-balance he watched in dismay as his shot came back off the cross bar. Harris then went close on three more occasions, Lucas Neill and substitute Kim Grant were also narrowly off-target and Walker made a vital point-blank stop from Richard Sadlier.

Millwall's failure to kill off their opponents served only to raise the tension on the terraces and on the bench as the final minutes approached. Sensing that they were still in the tie, Walsall mounted a final push and the ball pinged around the Lions goalmouth for what seemed an eternity. Then, with the job almost done, The Saddlers grabbed a dramatic last-minute equaliser when Eyjolffson got free at the far post to head home. Fortunately, there was little time left for Walsall to cause

Walsall 1	Millwall 1	**Referee:** David Pugh (Wirral)
Eyjolffson	*Sadlier*	

'We're off to Wembley.' Players celebrate over their victory against Walsall.

Millwall further embarrassment, and Mr Pugh's final whistle was greeted by a wave of relief and tears of joy from the South London contingent.

1998/99:

P	W	D	L	F	A	PTS
46	17	11	18	52	59	62

Division Two
Tenth Place
Joint Managers: Keith Stevens/Alan McLeary
Top Goalscorer: Neil Harris (18)
Highest Attendance: Manchester City 12,726
Average Attendance: 6,959

THE SADDLER
Millwall issue

Tuesday, 16th March 1999
Auto Windscreens Shield
Southern Area Final 2nd Leg
Kick Off: 7.45pm
Price: £1.80p

Target: Wembley

Club Sponsor
BANKS'S

Match Sponsor
YALE EDDISON LIFT TRUCK SERVICES

Matchball Sponsor
STEVE PLATT COMMERCIALS

Walsall: Walker, Marsh, Pointon (Evans 82), Keates (Thomas 73),Viveash, Roper, Wrack, Cramb, Brissett, Larusson, Mavrak, (Eyjolfsson 61).
Millwall: Roberts, Lavin, Stuart, Bowry, Nethercott, Dolan, Ifill (Grant 64), Newman, Harris (Bircham 90), Sadlier, Neill. Sub not used: Smith.

MILLWALL v. ROTHERHAM UNITED

7 April 2001   Football League Nationwide Division Two
The New Den   Attendance: 16,015

The new Millennium season gave Millwall something to look forward to. They had just missed out on promotion by losing in the play-offs. They had kept their young team together and Neil Harris was scoring for fun having netted 25 times before this encounter. Joint managers Keith Stevens and Alan McLeary were sacked in September but by then the fight and determination had been installed into these talented youngsters. Matty Lawrence was the only regular first-team player signed to shore up the defence and with Sean Dyche back from injury, replacing Joe Dolan who broke his leg midway through the season, the back four were settled. Mark McGhee was to replace Rhino and Macca and had to push the team forward for promotion with the aid of assistant Steve Gritt. Just before the transfer deadline Millwall suffered injuries to their forwards Harris and Moody and quickly lined up Tony Cottee and Steve Claridge for the remainder of the season.

When The Lions met Rotherham it was first versus second with Rotherham level on points and with a game in hand. Having been beaten in December at Millmoor by three goals to two, Millwall were expecting a very tough game. Leading scorer Harris was missing from the line-up and was replaced by veteran Claridge. And what a replacement he was, as Millwall gave United a lesson in football winning 4-0 and Man of the Match Claridge getting two. The hosts totally overwhelmed their visitors in the opening exchanges and raced into an early 12th minute lead when midfielder Tim Cahill converted Richard Sadlier's flick for his eighth goal of the season. Millwall kept up the pressure and nearly went further in front when the Australian came close again. Tony Warner made a magnificent save from Mark Robbins when he tipped the ball over the bar. But midway through the half Rotherham 'keeper Ian Gray was beaten for a second time when a quick free-kick was floated into the area. Dyche's effort was blocked right into Reid's path, and he made no mistake from the edge of the area to double the lead. Rotherham's plight

Sean Dyche's (left) and Stuart Nethercott's (right) pairing in defence was one of the main reasons Milwall gained promotion. Dyche was signed from Chesterfield and Nethercott from Spurs.

Millwall 4   **Rotherham Utd 0**   **Referee:** Dermot Gallagher
  Cahill   (Banbury)
  Reid
  Claridge (2)

Neil Harris is hugged by Tony Warner who ran to the halfway line to celebrate Neil's goal.

went from bad to worse when they were reduced to ten men after Alan Lee was sent off for a second bookable offence, and moments later Richard Sadlier's looping header hit the bar and Claridge was on hand to head his first goal for the club. After the restart, Millwall were just as emphatic and completed the rout when Claridge chipped home from 25 yards to seal the points.

Rotherham's manager Ronnie Moore commented: 'It was very painful and embarrassing, we were fortunate that they didn't score more goals. That side will go on and win the division and don't let Mark McGhee kid you that it's not over yet. Millwall are the best side by a mile.'

2000/01:

P	W	D	L	F	A	PTS	GD
46	28	9	9	89	38	93	51

Division Two
Champions
Manager: Mark McGhee
Top Goalscorer: Neil Harris (28)
Highest Attendance: Oldham 18,510
Average Attendance: 11,443

Millwall: Warner, Lawrence (Kinet), Nethercott, Dyche, Ryan, Ifilll, Cahill, Livermore, Reid, Sadlier, Claridge.

Rotherham: Gray, Watson, Artell, Branston, Bryan (Sedgwick), Scott, Talbot, Hurst, Warner, Robins (Barker), Lee.

Millwall v. Oldham

6 May 2001   Nationwide League Division Two
The New Den   Attendance: 18,510

Millwall already knew that they were promoted after drawing at Wrexham the previous week, but needed a win to make sure of the championship. Raucous rock music, balloons and confetti got the Millwall fans in the mood to party and The Lions turned on a champagne performance to breeze past Oldham. Choruses of 'Cheer up Mark McGhee' and 'Let 'em all come down to The Den', set the game underway in the spring sunshine.

In the first twenty minutes, flooding the midfield with five players, Oldham set out to stifle Millwall and always looked dangerous on the counter attack. But Neil Harris, who is clearly a player who belongs at the top level, used his hunger and guile to get himself free on the left on 21 minutes to send in a glorious ball for Paul Moody to convert from close range. Nine minutes later and Harris was put through, but instead of squaring to the unmarked David Livermore, he hit the most sublime chip over Gary Kelly to put Millwall in total control.

Oldham might have hoped that with the game practically sewn up at half-time Millwall would just coast to victory. But the Lions showed why they are the best side in the division with an inspired performance in the second period. Moody hit the bar and then Harris dragged a shot just wide before Steven Reid scored one of the best goals of the season, after Harris laid the ball back to Reid on the edge of the area for the twenty-year-old hit a thunderous shot that crashed home via the underside of the bar.

It was a strike that left McGhee to admit afterwards it was the best finish he had ever seen. The only Millwall player still showing the nerves that were evident in the opening twenty minutes was 'keeper Tony Warner, who dropped a John Sheridan free-kick at the feet of Barry Prenderville – who somehow shot wide with the goal at his mercy. It took the fourth strike for the crowd to really start their celebrations when Harris crossed again for the thirty-three-year-old Moody to plant his header home for his 14th goal of the season.

Warner made amends for his earlier blunder when he saved brilliantly from Oldham substitute Mark Allott's shot, but it was left to Harris to have the final say in the game after Sheridan had needlessly brought down Lion's substitute Marc Bircham in the final minute for the Millwall hitman to calmly slot home his 27th League goal of the season from the penalty spot.

The final whistle sounded on an momentous campaign for Millwall and the celebrations began with the presentation of the championship trophy. Oldham manager Andy Ritchie admitted his team had lost out to a far superior side. He said, 'There is no doubt Millwall are the best side in the League and deserve to go up as champions'.

Proudly wearing his championship gold medal, McGhee said, 'We think we've got a good squad here with a lot of ability still to come out. I feel we are only touching on it. I have been able to develop and take advantage of what was already in place at the club, there was no pressure today for the players but this will give them a great lesson for the future. It shows them what a great feeling it is to be champions and I have got no doubt they will be ready to go next season'. As for Reid's devastating goal, McGhee declared, 'I have played all over the world and I have never seen a better finish. He can get better and better.'

Millwall 5   **Oldham Athletic 0**   **Referee:** A. Bates (Stoke)
  Moody (2)
  Harris (2, 1 pen)
  Reid

Neil Harris who scored two goals in this match was leading goal scorer at Millwall with 27 goals. He was signed from Cambridge City.

Paul Moody mobbed after scoring one of his 12 goals that season. He was signed from Fulham.

Millwall: Warner, Lawrence, Nethercott, Dyche, Ryan; Neill, Livermore, Cahill, (Bircham), Reid, (Kinet); Harris, Moody.

Oldham Athletic: Kelly, Garnett, (Allott), McNiven, Futcher, Prenderville, Duxbury, Sheridan, Rickers, Carss, Parkin, Corazzin, (Roach)

WATFORD v. MILLWALL

1 January 2002
Vicarage Road, Watford

Nationwide League Division One
Attendance: 15,300

Many matches are described as classics for various reasons, and this encounter for the purist would not come into that category, but the 3,000 Millwall supporters who witnessed the event would no doubt use the word unsparingly, as they saw their hero Neil Harris score in his rehabilitation match after his successful fight against testicular cancer.

Neil had missed pre-season training, after he had been diagnosed with the dreadful disease in June and after a brief spell in the side in September he suffered a setback that put his recovery trip hold for a while, with the holiday period pencilled in as a possible comeback.

Millwall entered their third festive game on the back of two home wins, against Palace and Crewe, and so entered Vicarage Road in fifth spot with very high hopes. They were pitting their wits against one of the early-season favourites, now led by Gianluca Vialli, the former Chelsea manager and Italian international.

This was the first meeting of the campaign between the two sides, as the Lions' home game against the Hornets had been twice postponed, the second due to an impromptu bonfire in a works unit close to The Den back in October. Millwall therefore didn't really know what to expect from Vialli's highly experienced team.

Any fears within the Lions contingent were soon dispelled as rampant Millwall completely dominated Watford to such an extent that there was no comparison between the two sides. Despite the away side's dominance, Tommy Smith nearly gave the home team the lead after 25 minutes when striking a Millwall post.

But when the Lions scored seven minutes later there only going to be one winner. Steve Claridge, Richard Sadlier, and the exciting Steven Reid, set up Tim Cahill to head home the opener, after he had timed his run into the area to perfection. This strike should have been the Australian's second goal as after 16 minutes of play he had shot straight at Alec Chamberlain when well placed.

The surprise to many was that the second Millwall goal didn't arrive until the 59th minute when Sadlier reacted first to a Marc Bircham shot to rifle the ball past Chamberlain, and nine minutes later it was the excellent Reid who ran free onto a long pass from Matt Lawrence to shoot home hard and low for the third through the 'keeper's legs.

This virtually sewed up the game for Millwall, although Heidar Helguson pulled one back for the demoralised Hornets after 82 minutes, shortly after Tony Warner had saved from Wooter's point blank effort. It was to be 'Bomber' Harris who would have the last word when, with three minutes left to play, the Lions hero replaced Steve Claridge.

Harris restored the three-goal margin with a typical stunning effort that is one of his trademarks: picking up the ball out wide he turned Pierre Issa inside-out to send a curling drive into the far corner of the net from the edge of the area, much to the joy of his team-mates who all gathered to hoist the goalscorer in celebration.

This was the game in which the Lions peaked, and would go on to finish a more-than-successful campaign by qualifying for the play-offs. Sad Watford's day was completed when Vega was sent off in injury time for tugging at Sadlier's shirt.

Watford 1	Millwall 4	Referee: C.J. Foy (Merseyside)
Helguson	*Cahill*	
	Sadlier, Reid	
	Harris	

Cancer agony of Millwall hotshot

by Greg Fidgeon

MILLWALL striker Neil Harris is likely to miss the whole of next season after being diagnosed with testicular cancer.

Harris, who lives in Rayleigh, led the south London club to the Division Two title last season with a 28-goal haul which led to him being awarded the golden boot.

A press statement from the club said: "Millwall are devastated to report Neil Harris has been diagnosed with testicular cancer.

"He underwent surgery on Friday (June 1) and we await the result of further tests. We are hopeful that Neil will make a full recovery – but it is unlikely that he will play next season."

The former Great Wakering Rovers and Maldon striker only discovered he had the disease on Thursday and underwent surgery the following day.

Club chairman Theo Paphitis rates Harris highly and told the club's website: "We brought him on, we coached him and he's given some incredible performances on the pitch.

"He's entertained and he's been a key figure in our promotion charge."

Harris, who signed an improved contract with the club last week, was already planning for next season and he told the club's website: "We see the Second Division championship as the start of something bigger, and we're realistically looking for a top six finish in Division One next season."

Harris will now has to hope his team mates turn his words into a reality as he spends the season recuperating.

The press statement continued: "Clearly this has come as a major shock to himself, his family, friends and all associated with Millwall.

"We would ask that everyone respect Neil's need for privacy and understanding at this time."

Harris joined Millwall from non-league Cambridge City and has scored over 70 goals for the club.

His prowess in front of goal has seen him linked with big-money moves to the Premier League with Tottenham Hotspur, Charlton Athletic, Ipswich Town and Coventry City all rumoured to be interested.

Scotland boss Craig Brown and Republic of Ireland manager Mick McCarthy were also said to be checking his eligibility for their respective nations.

STAR: Neil Harris in action for Millwall this season

Millwall's triumphant promotion celebrations of 2001 were cut short when the news broke of leading goalscorer Neil Harris' fight against testicular cancer in late May of that year. Press coverage of this shock announcement was fairly extensive, as shown in this report.

2001/02:

P	W	D	L	F	A	PTS
46	22	11	13	69	48	77

Division One
Manager: Mark McGhee
Top Goalscorer: Steve Claridge (17)
Highest Attendance: Wolverhampton Wanderers 17,058
Average Attendance: 13,253

'I was pleased for Neil Harris, and the whole team's reaction said a lot. That was a very special moment for everybody.'
Mark McGhee

Watford: Chamberlain, Blondeau, Issa (Wooter), Vega, Robinson (Cox), Nielsen, Fisken, Vernazza, Helguson, Gayle, Smith (Noel-Williams).
Millwall: Warner, Lawrence, Nethercott, Dyche, Ryan, Reid, Bircham, Cahill, Livermore, Sadlier, Claridge (Harris).

Team spirit after Neil Harris gets his first goal at Watford in 4-1 victory.